THE BLACK PLACE TWO SEASONS

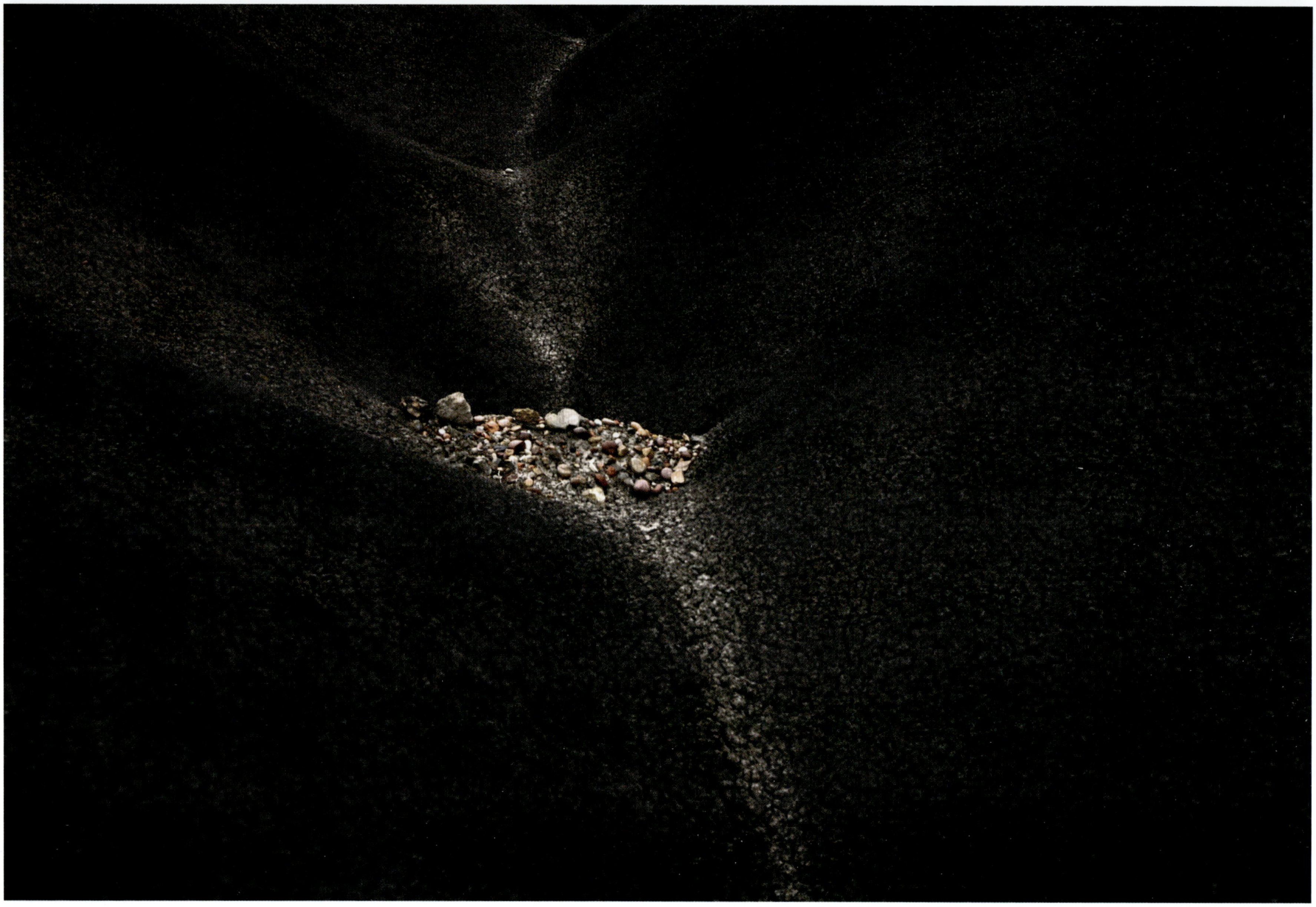

THE BLACK PLACE TWO SEASONS

PHOTOGRAPHS BY WALTER W. NELSON

INTRODUCTION BY KATHERINE WARE

ESSAY BY DOUGLAS PRESTON

MUSEUM OF NEW MEXICO PRESS, SANTA FE

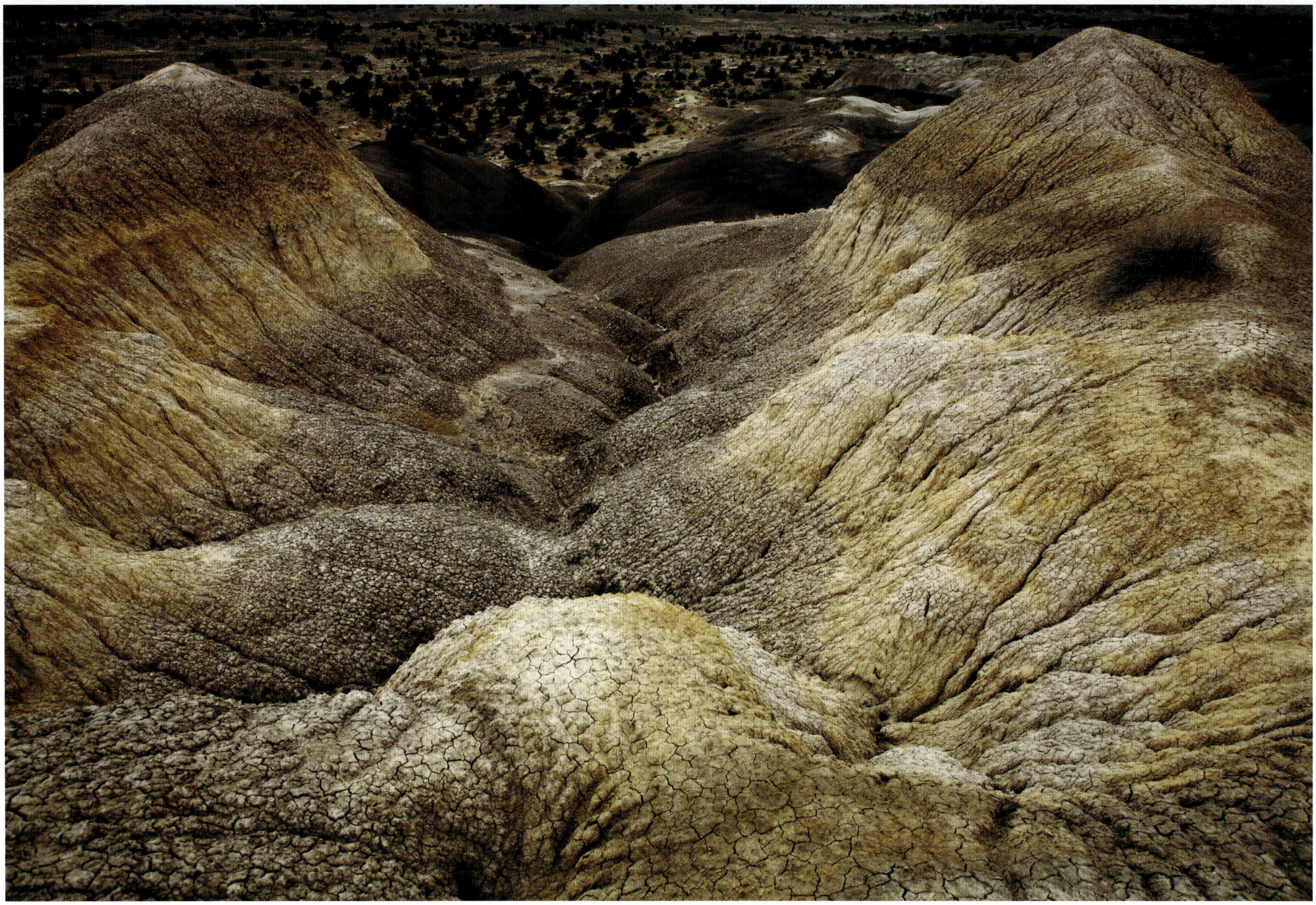

CONTENTS

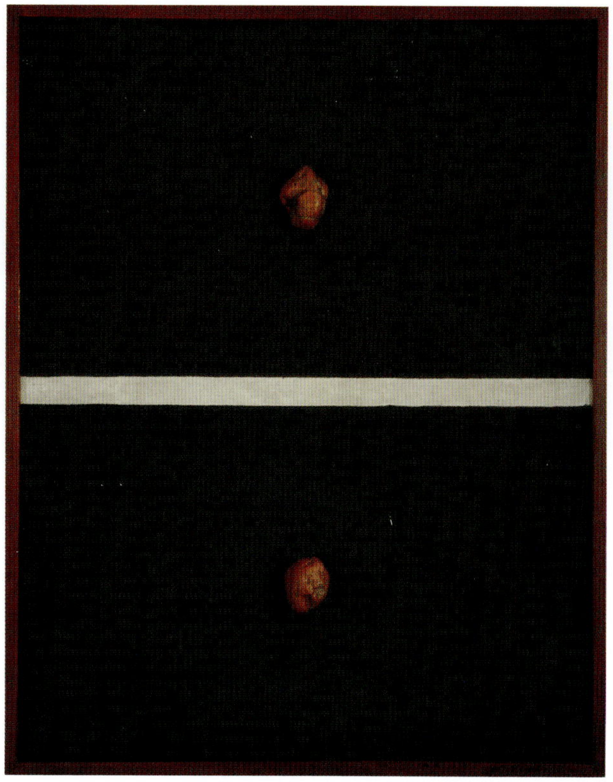
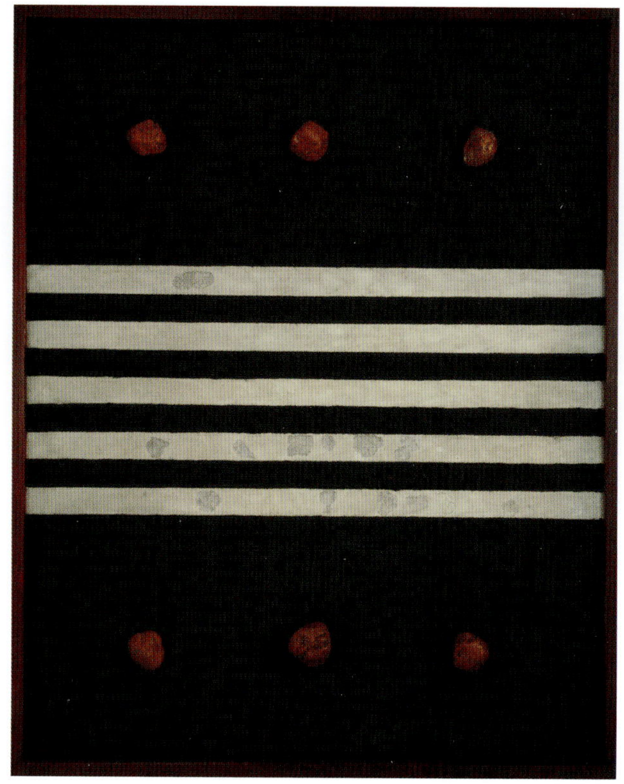
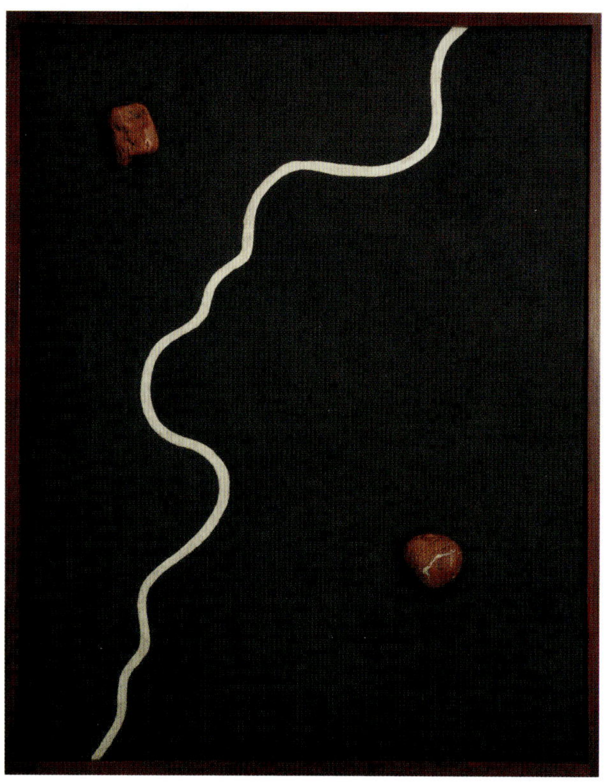
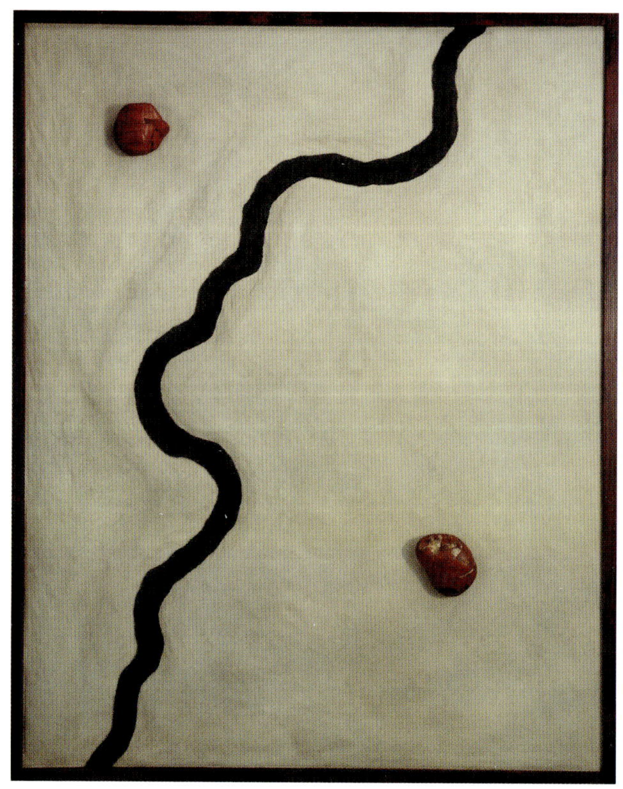

ARTIST STATEMENT

WALTER W. NELSON

WHILE LIVING IN NEW YORK CITY in the late 1970s and early 1980, I began my journey into the fine arts—photography, painting, and sculpture. A strong part of my evolutionary development as an artist came from reading about the lives of artists, especially Georgia O'Keeffe. Her journey of discovery to the Southwest and her transformation as an artist there guided me to New Mexico in 1982. I started a visual quest to locate some of the areas in which O'Keeffe painted. After spending considerable time photographing and painting in these areas, I went in search of the most mystical of her locations: the mysterious landscape she called the Black Place. This is where she painted some of her greatest landscape paintings, a place that transformed her vision as an artist. After much searching, I found the Black Place in the remote badlands of the Navajo Indian Reservation and was able to locate the exact formations she painted.

Today the Black Place remains a remote and uninhabited landscape known only to a few. It is one of the harshest places in the lower forty-eight states—bitterly cold in winter, baking hot in summer, devoid of life, swept by ferocious winds, receiving less than four inches of rain a year.

The title of this book, *The Black Place—Two Seasons,* comes from the fact that there are only two visual seasons in the Black Place. The first, spring–summer–fall, reveals a landscape of sun, wind, and heat. And then there is winter, when snow, sculpted by violent winds sweeping across earth forms, transforms the black formations into something otherworldly and utterly beyond words.

In the past twenty years I have returned to the Black Place more than thirty times, sometimes spending days on end, photographing in large-format 8 x 10 black-and-white and in digital color. Color in this black-and-white landscape adds to the mystical beauty and austerity of the landforms. These photographs, in addition to their own vision, give the viewer the opportunity to connect to this place that was so central to Georgia O'Keeffe's growth as an artist, and they illuminate her stark, uncompromising vision.

As a multidisciplinary artist, within this body of work I have produced sculpture relief paintings from black and white earth and red jasper rocks found in the Black Place. I created these earth textures by grinding the earth and mixing it with a solution of damar resin, linseed oil, turpentine, and cobalt dryer to form a thick earth impasto. As an anchoring base for this impasto I used metal lathing in a wooden frame; the jasper is mounted on the surface. (Four such works are opposite.)

When one enters into the Black Place, one walks slowly in a meditative awareness looking for the gifts that lie within—these I give to you.

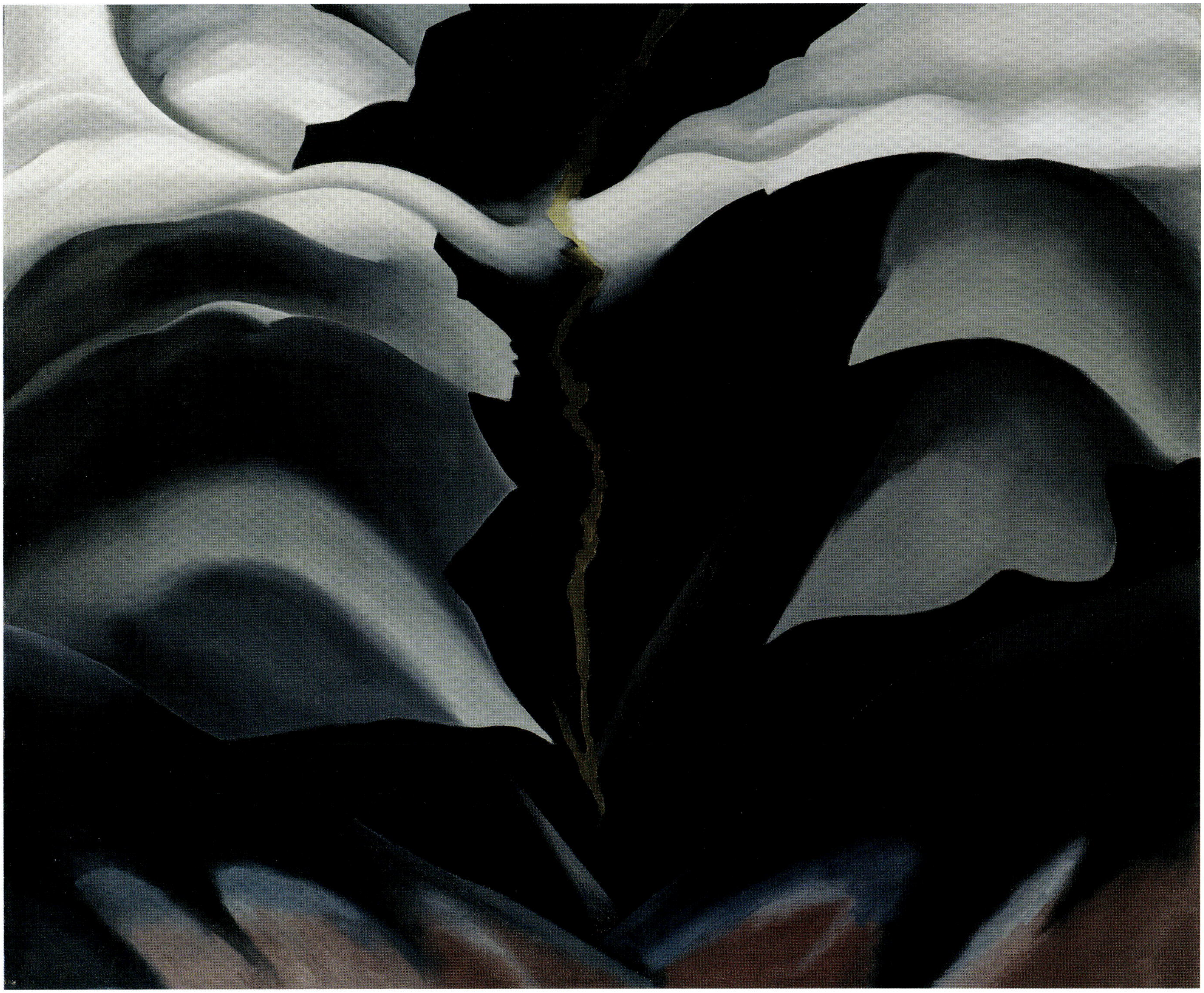

Georgia O'Keeffe, *Black Place II,* 1944.
Oil on canvas, 23⅞ x 30 inches, courtesy The Metropolitan Museum of Art.

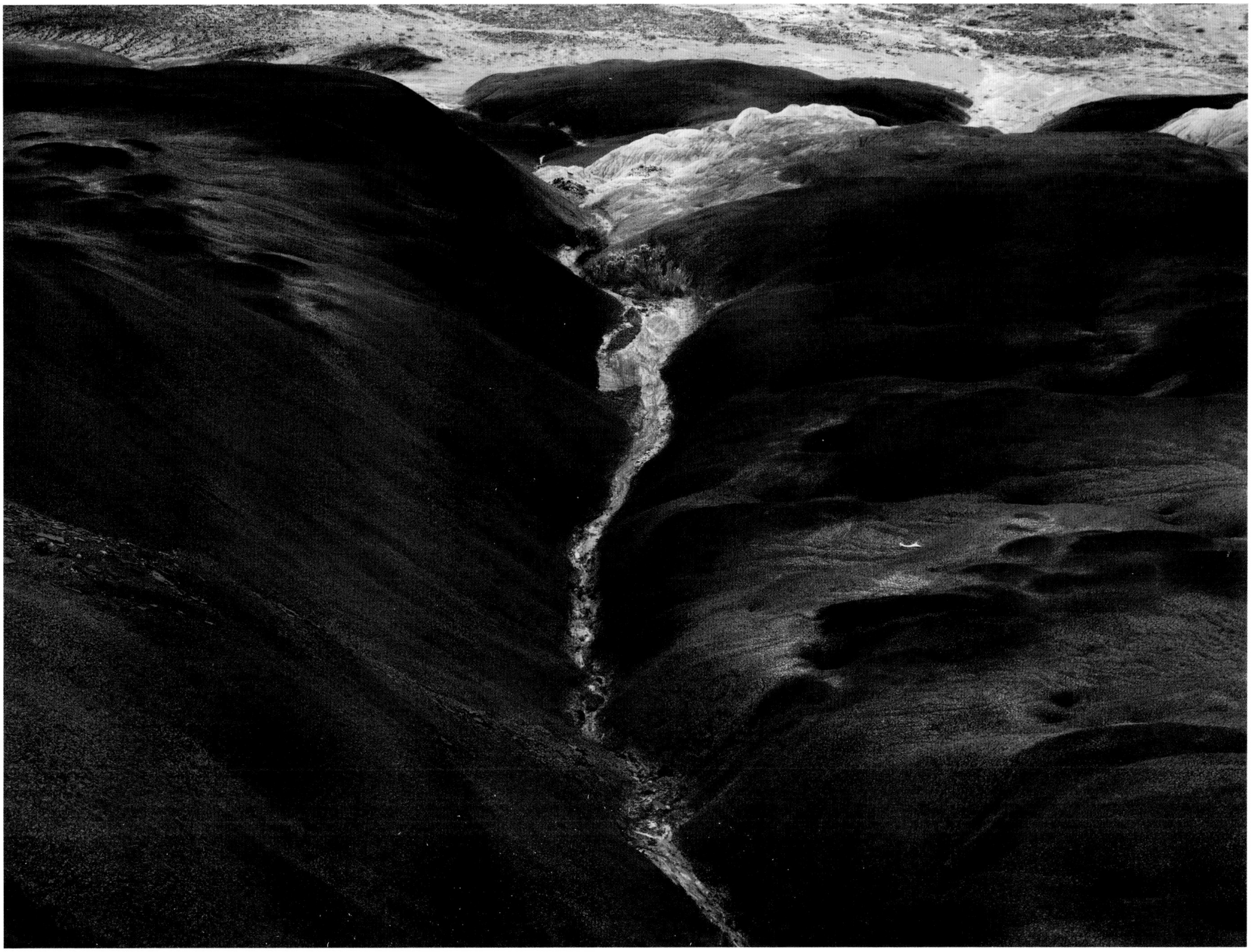

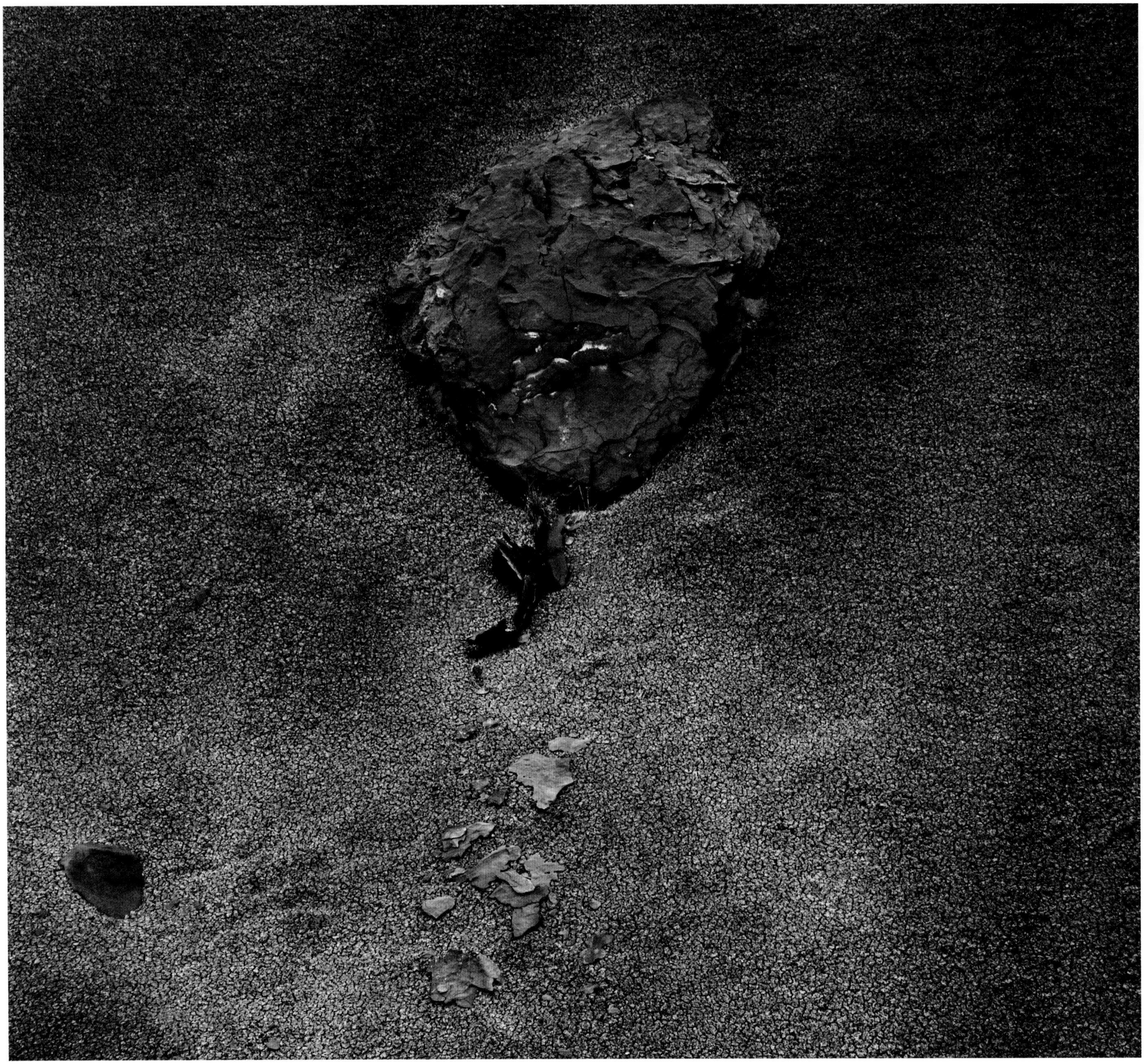

INTRODUCTION

KATHERINE WARE

A few decades after its inception, photography was quickly put to use in capturing images of faraway places, providing armchair travelers with virtual visits to the monuments of ancient civilizations in Egypt, China, and India, among other locations. The camera brought back real-life views of geographic wonders such as mountains, icebergs, deserts, and jungles. It was also used to catalog natural resources for mining and speculation, as in the American West. Then, too, some views were made as souvenirs for tourists, to be purchased and assembled into albums for study and entertainment. Eventually, travelers began carrying their own cameras to bring back images as evidence of their worldliness, establishing the vacation ritual of photographing famous sites.

Some of these places have become prescribed beauty spots, destinations to be photographed as a way of ticking them off a life list. But even with admission fees, crowds of visitors, and park service management, many of these locations retain a tremendous resonance that sparks something in the human breast. Surely each of us, in some special place, has had that expansive sensation that brings out an urge toward poetry or picture making, the hope of snatching from the air some semblance of the extraordinary experience. Yet what can a mere mortal with a camera hope to express about the astonishing megaliths at Stonehenge or the vertiginous maw of the Grand Canyon? So very often the results are disappointing and pedestrian. And so we have our bards.

Artist Walter Nelson has heeded the call to action in seeking to capture the essence of a remote area in northern New Mexico known in English as the Black Place. While for some it may seem a landscape easily dismissed ("there's nothing there!"), for Nelson there is much to see in its emptiness. Others have photographed here, often in black and white (as did Nelson initially), but none with his tender constancy. This suite of images, the result of repeated visits over many years, confirms the Black Place's inhospitality to life-forms in every season and vividly evokes the breadth and the intimacy, the monotony and the specificity of this place like no other.

Here, the earth's dry skin unfolds in undulating waves. Miles and miles of elephant hide, creased with experience and memory, are punctuated by small grace notes: a cache of smooth pebbles resting in a hollow; a vivid red stone reposing like an exposed organ; an ocher fist raised up against the sky; a cenotaph jutting from the snow. Along other stretches, the land oozes across the hills like pale icing, crusting and sparkling in the sun.

Few of us will discover the unique geography of the Black Place in person, for despite its rugged exterior, it is a private and fragile place. Nelson's task, therefore, is to summon its particulars for us, as well to induce the sense of being there. Traveling the uneven terrain, he guides us on an intense and disorienting journey in his own footsteps, using the view camera's rich detail to suggest a whole range of sensory experiences: the sound of the wind, the relentlessness of the sun, the crumble of earth, the faint scent of the air. Frequently photographing the ground at his feet, Nelson denies us the horizon line in many of the pictures. He fills our field of view with the shifting integument of the Black Place, immersing us in it until the outside world is forgotten. Though his camera ranges over its varied topography, Nelson's images do not attempt to summarize the Black Place. Instead, they offer glimpses of this extraordinary site, suggesting that its entirety cannot be contained on the page but only implied.

The Black Place is just about the right size for human contemplation: bigger than we are but expressed in earthly terms that we can almost begin to grasp. Perhaps there are only a few places left where a shared human experience is possible, where we face the raw elements before us and confront the stark mystery of creation. It seems a timeless landscape because it so far exceeds our own perception of time, in which our brief lives are so central. The shared realization is one of insignificance and of astonishment at the world around us, the fact that we are here to experience it, though fleetingly. The silence is so profound that one can almost hear the sands of time shifting.

SPRING SUMMER FALL

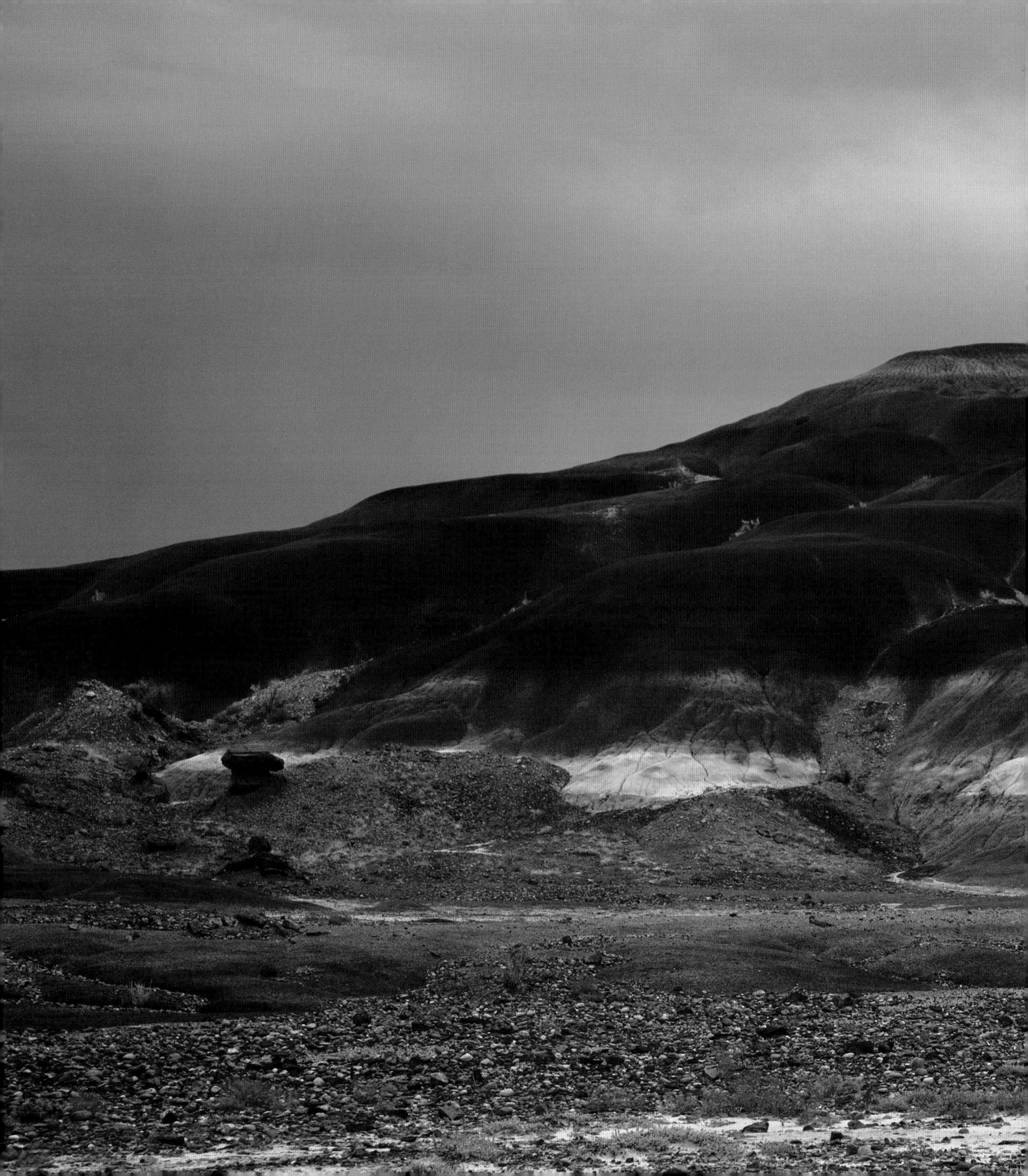

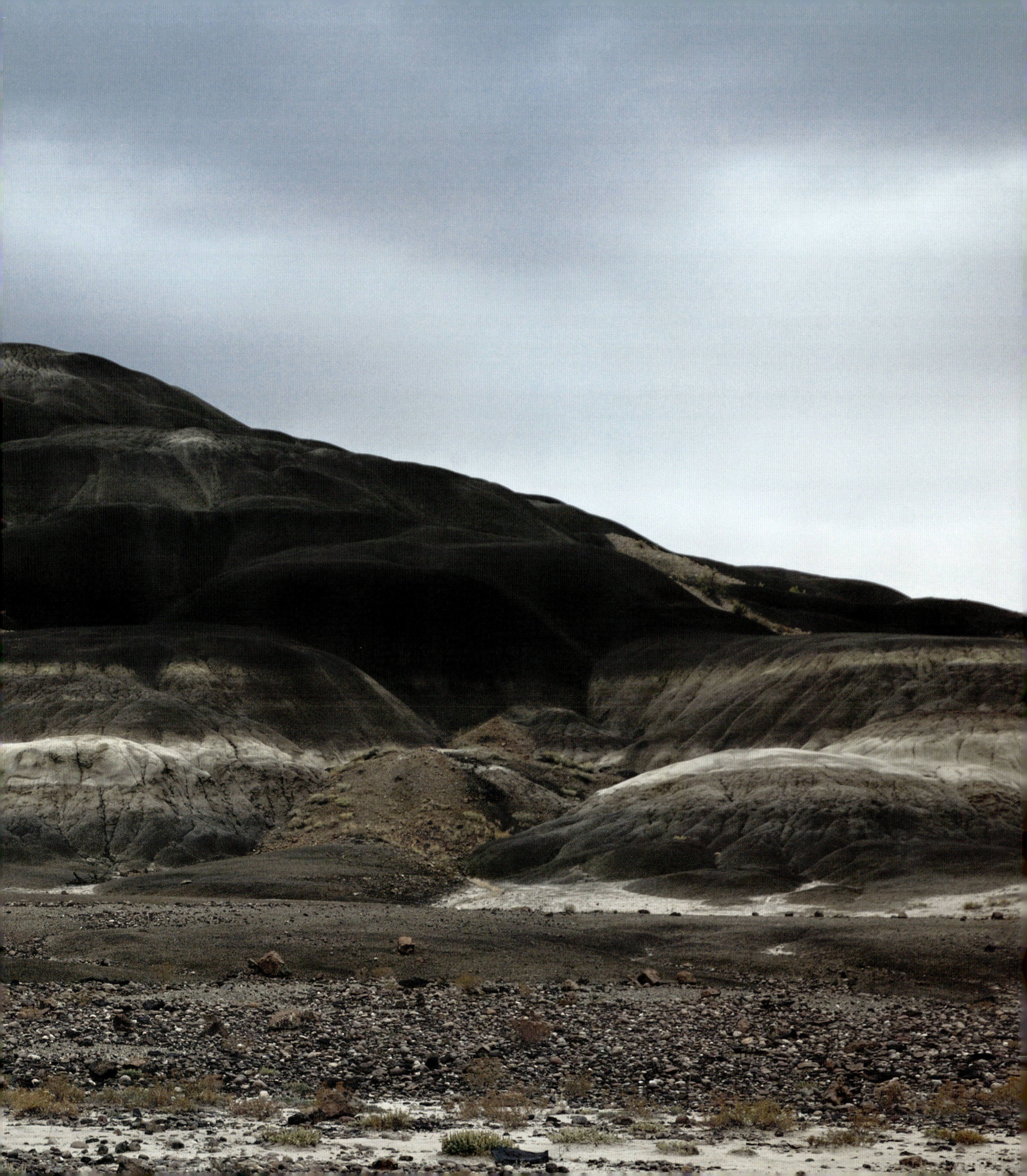

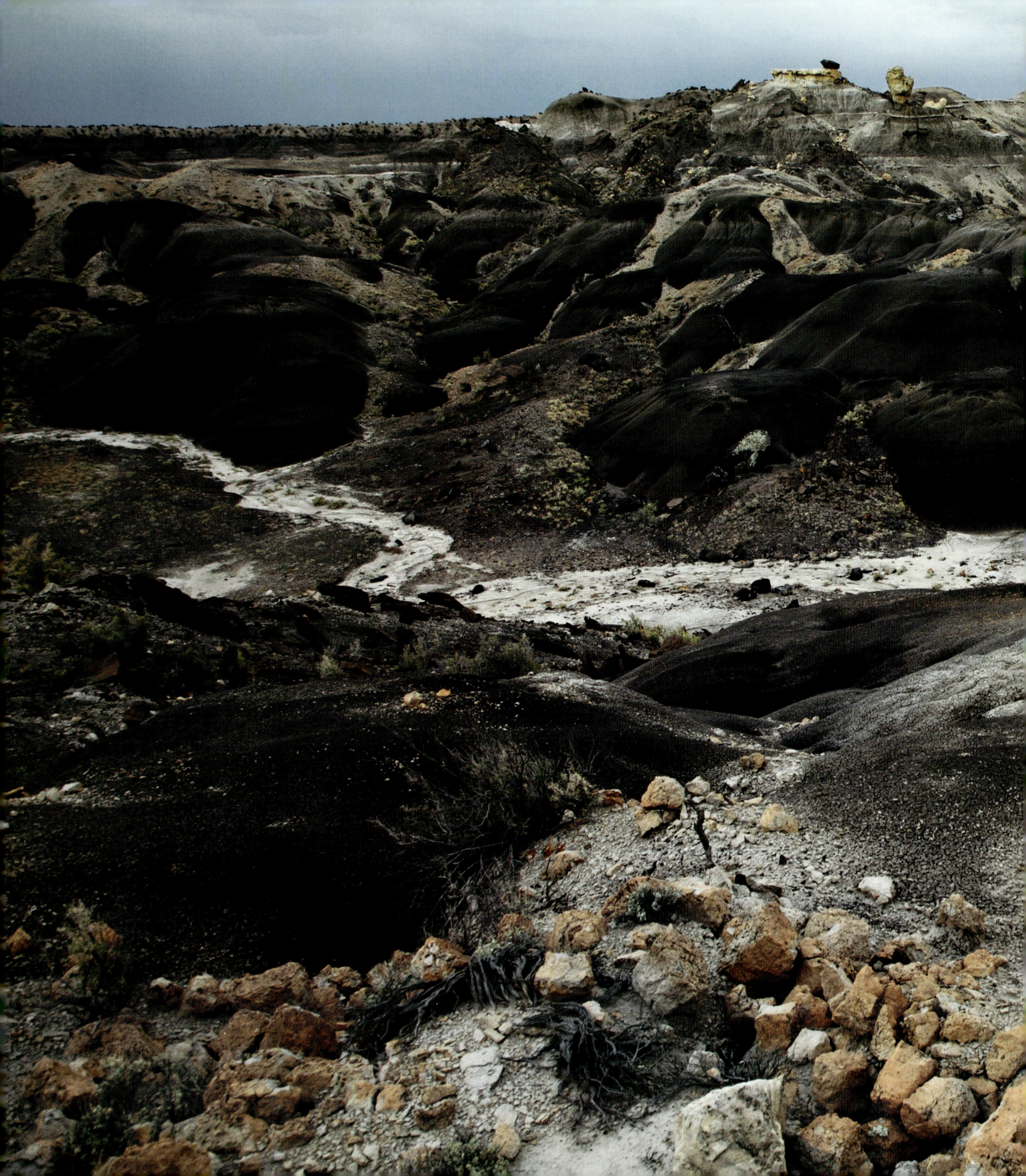

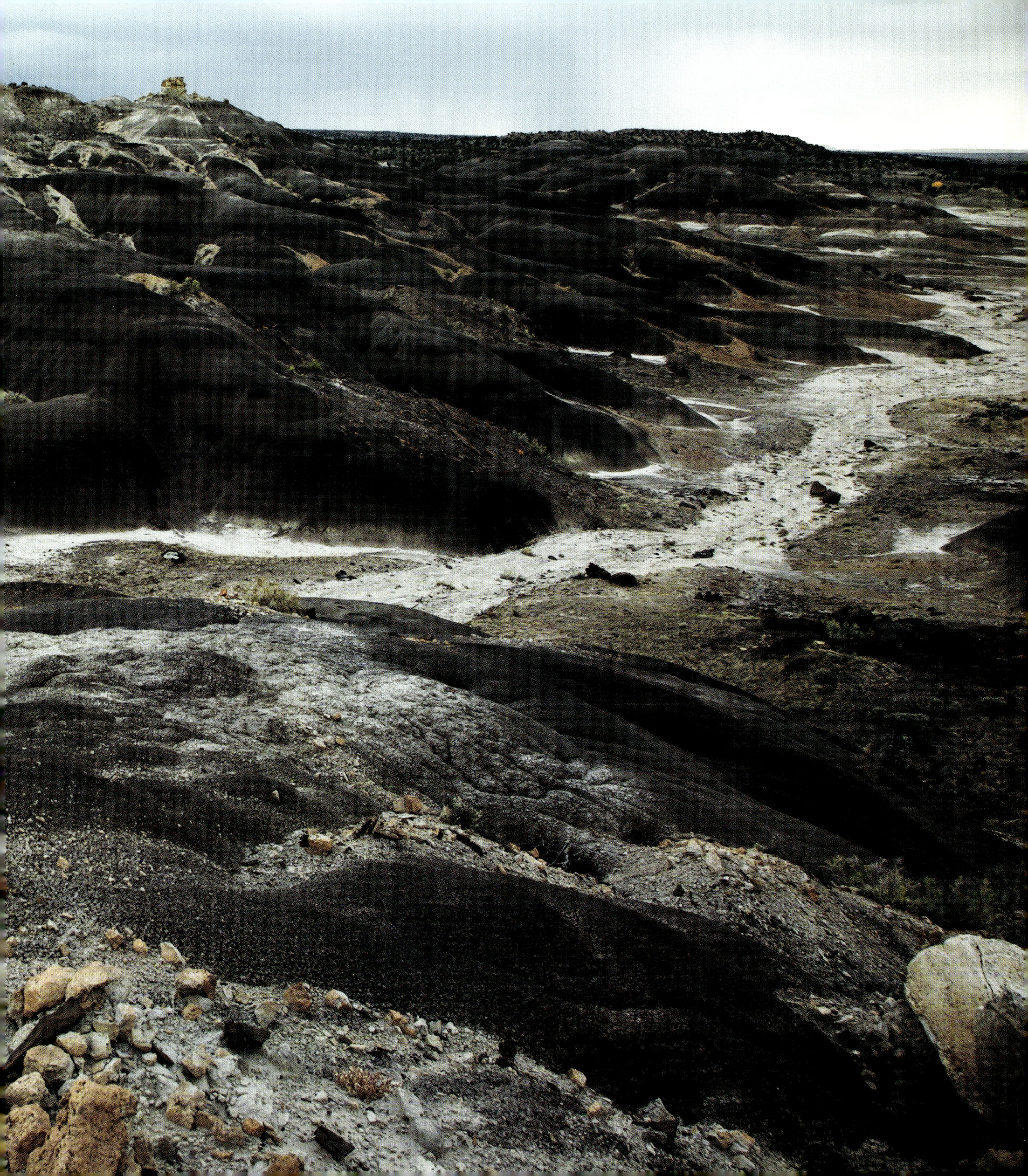

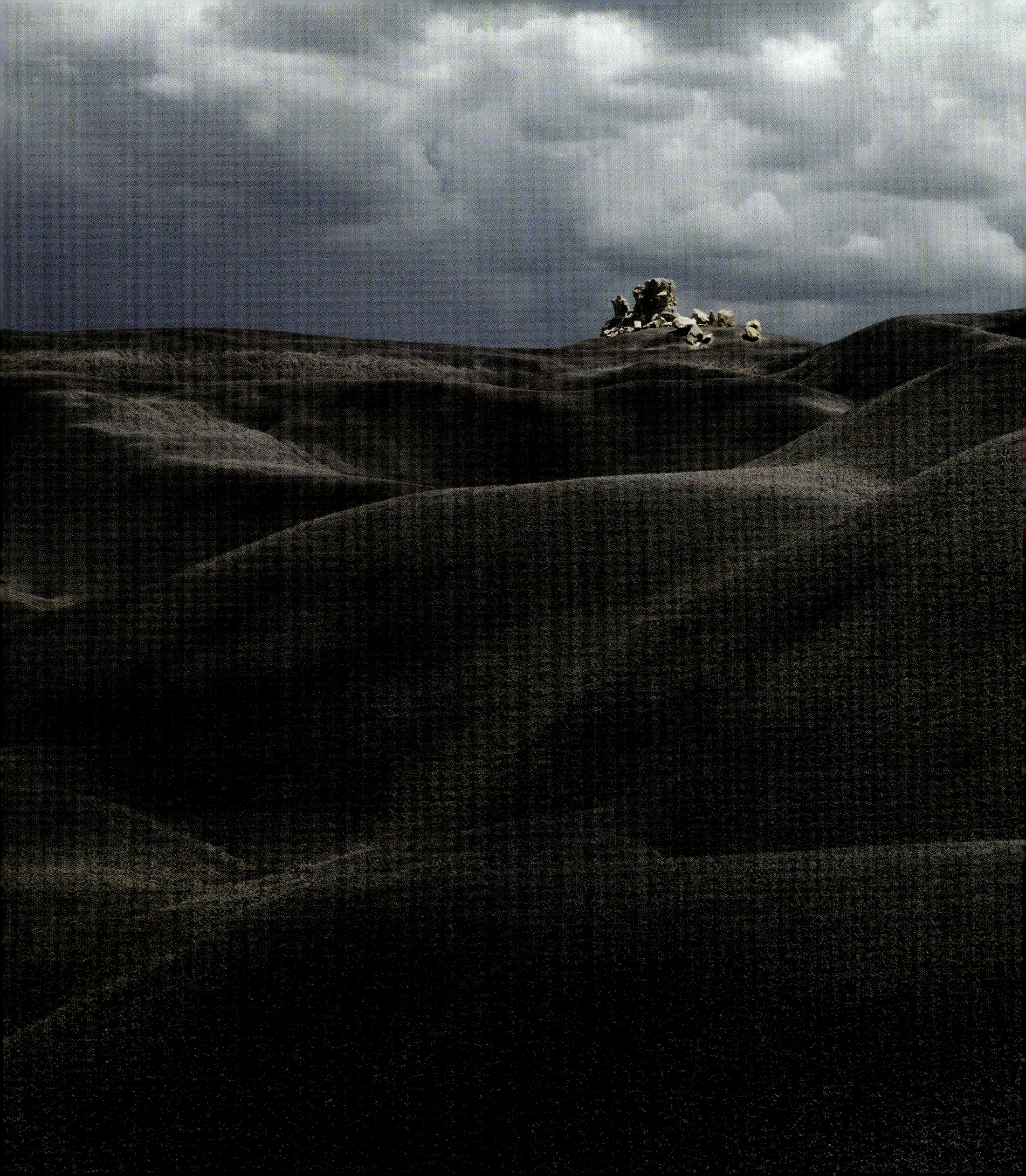

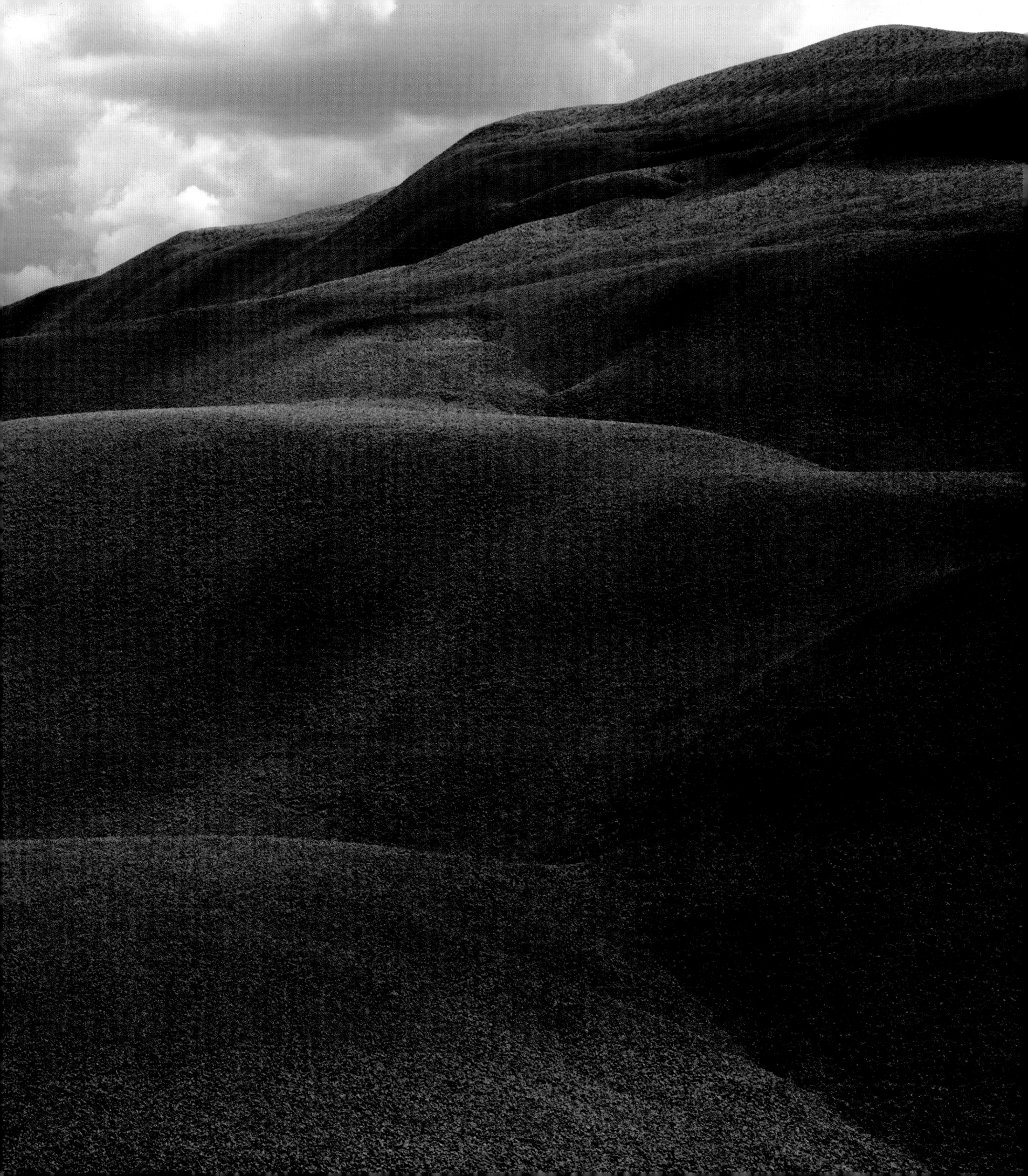

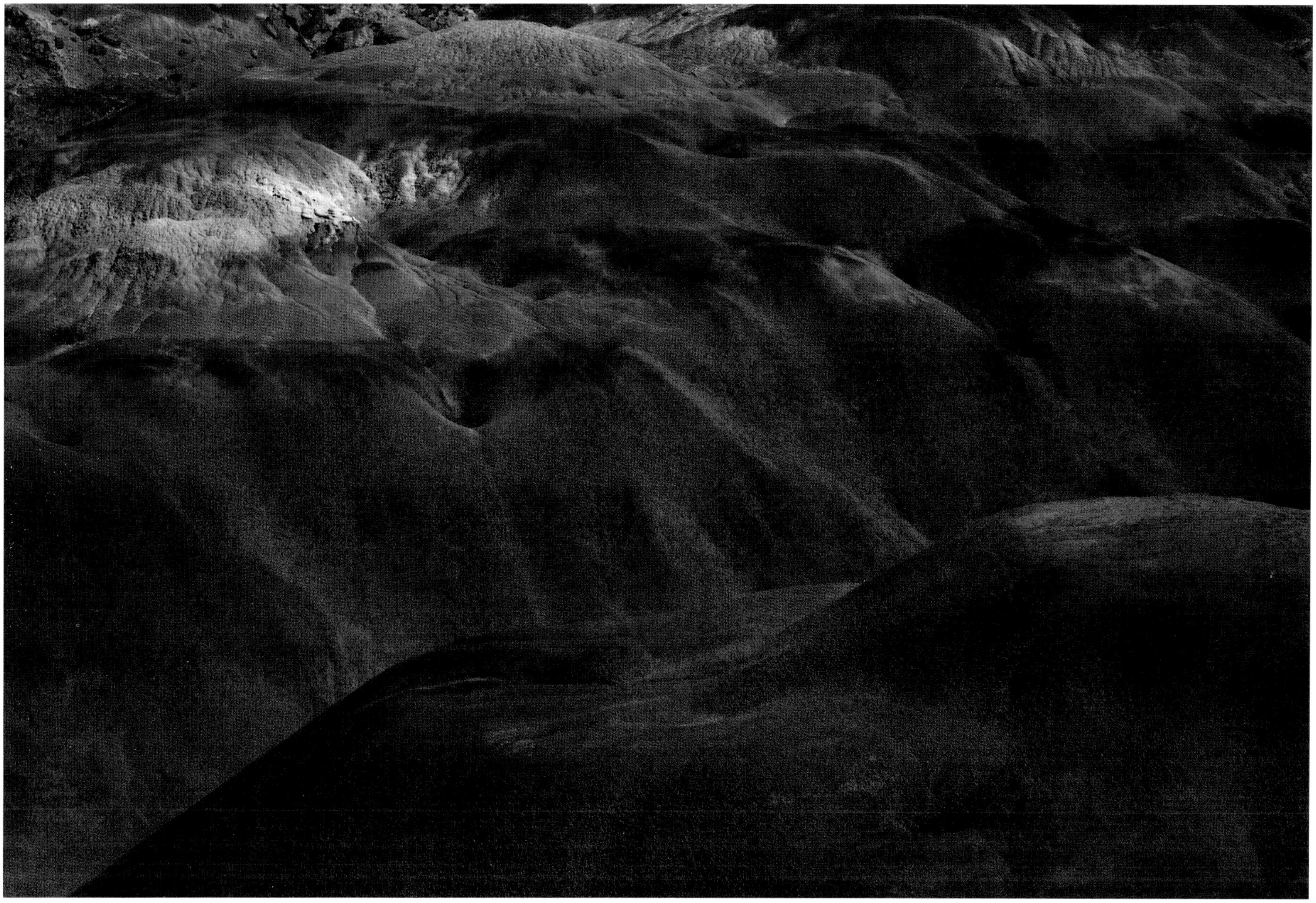

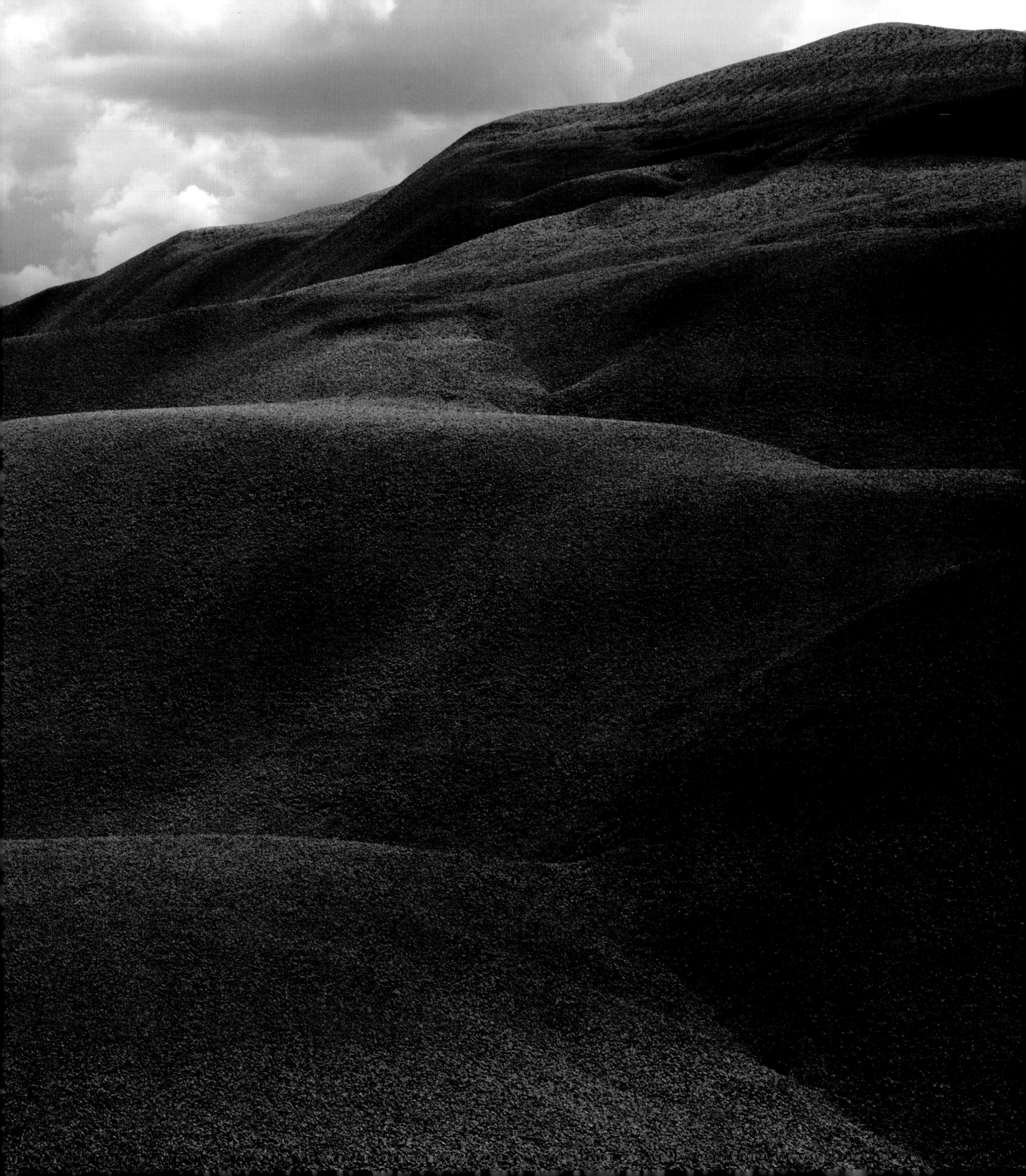

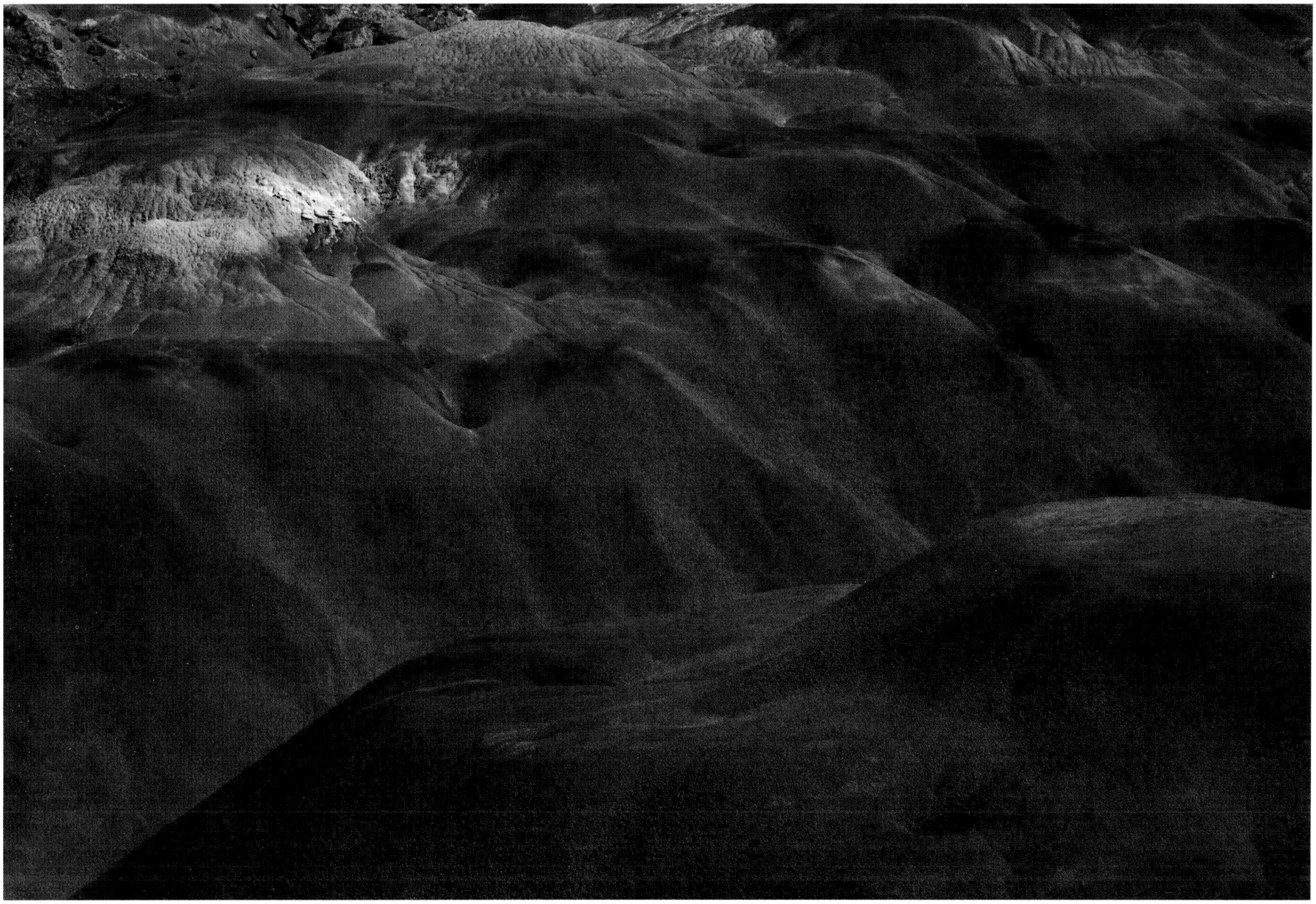

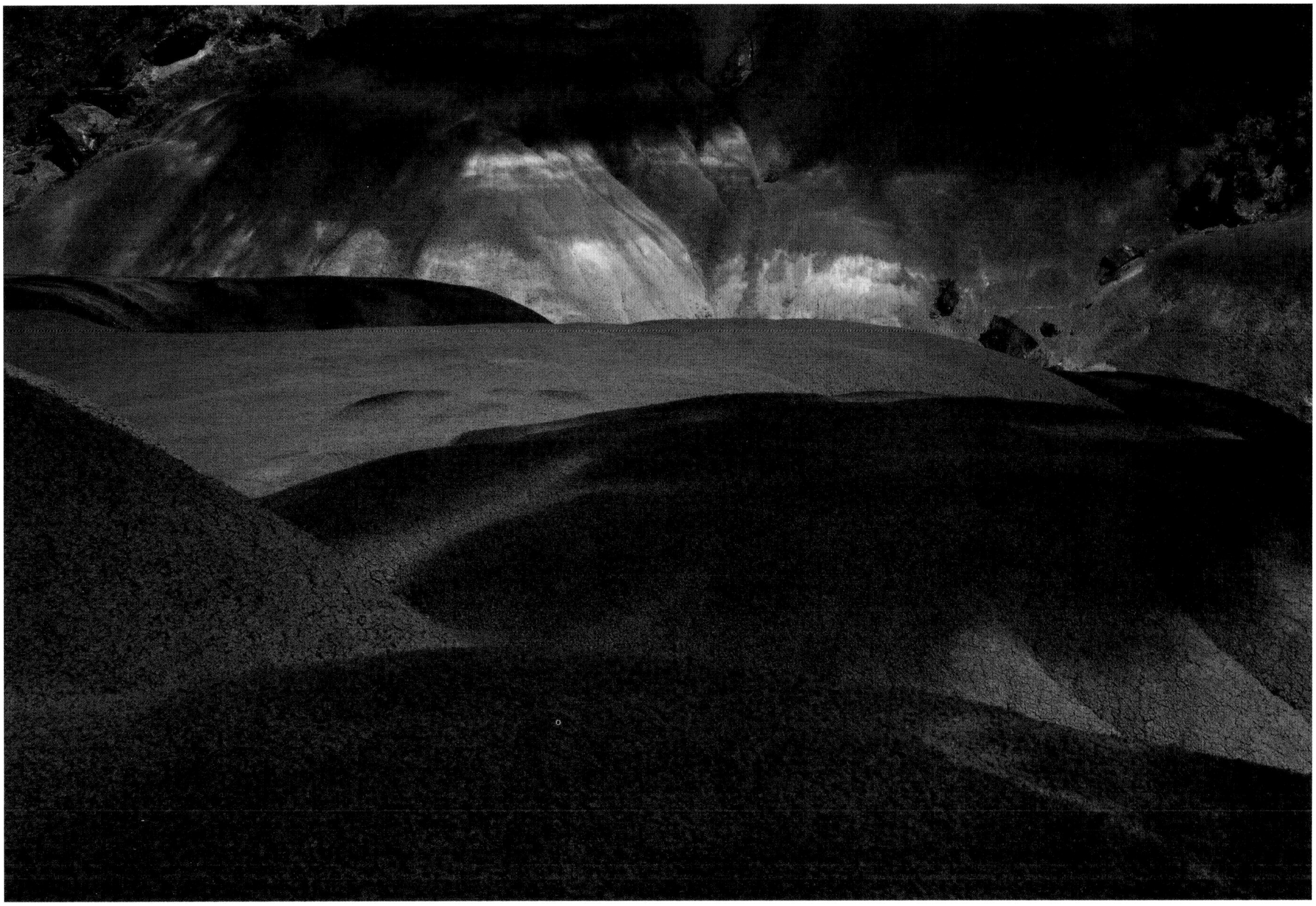

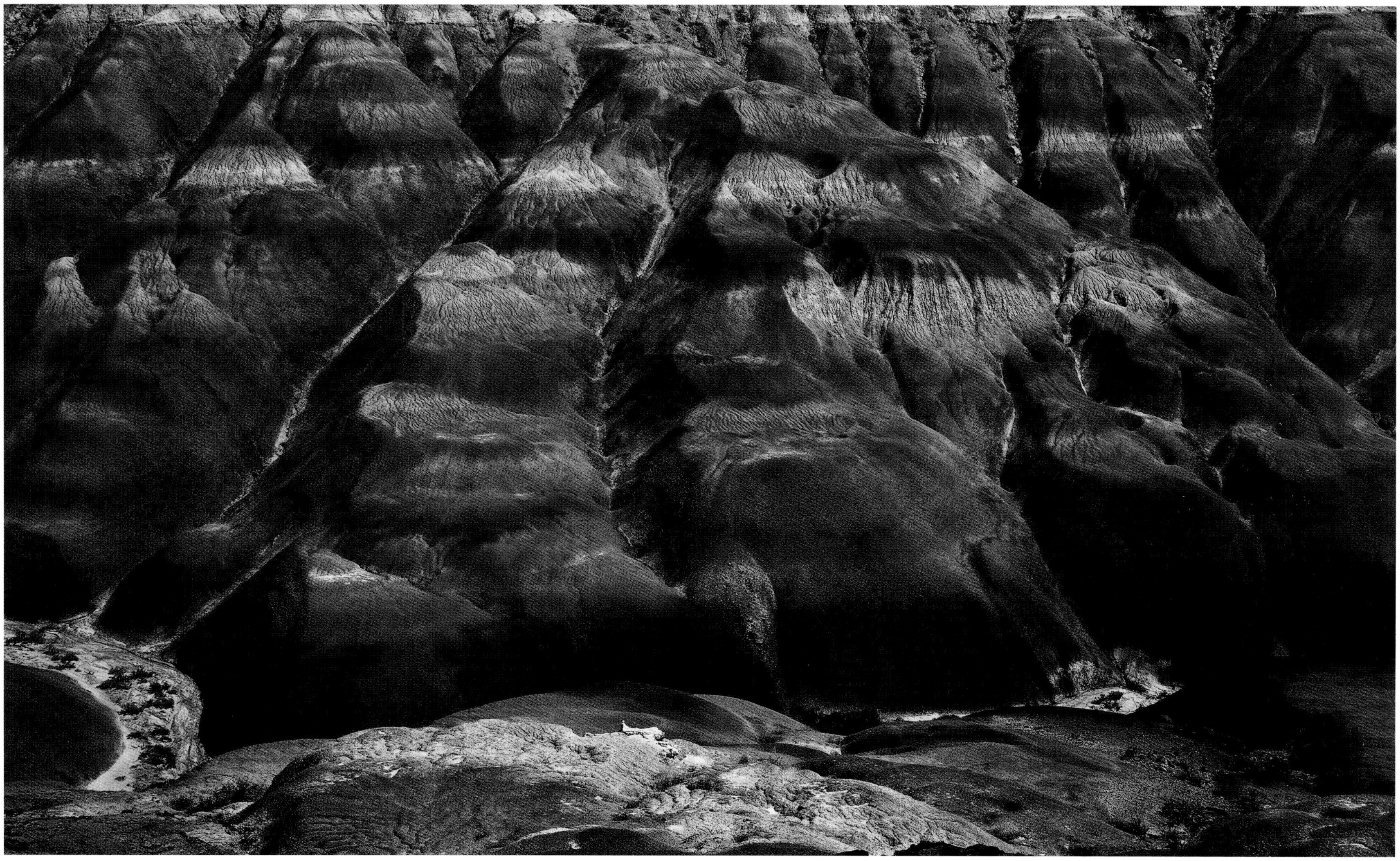

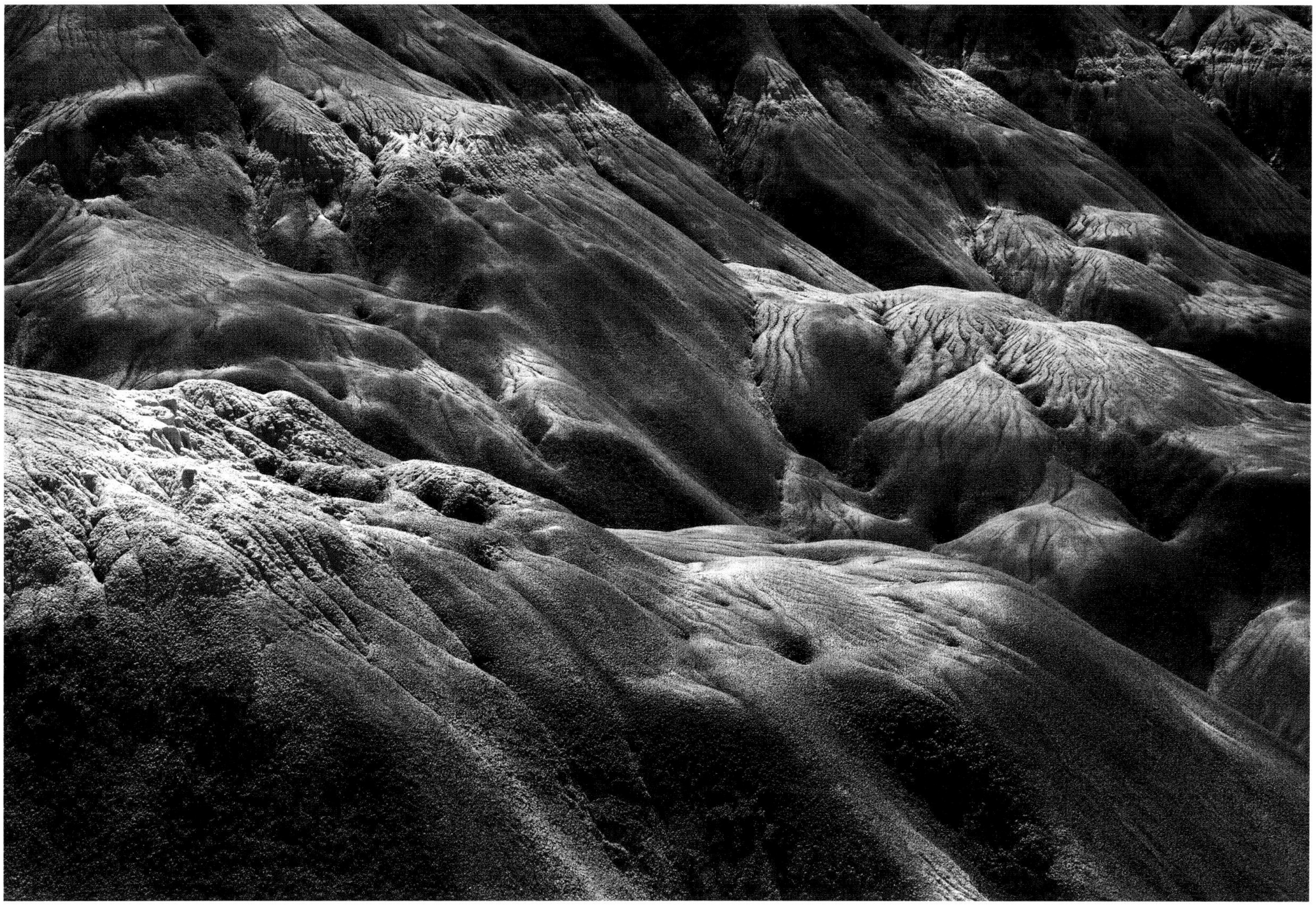

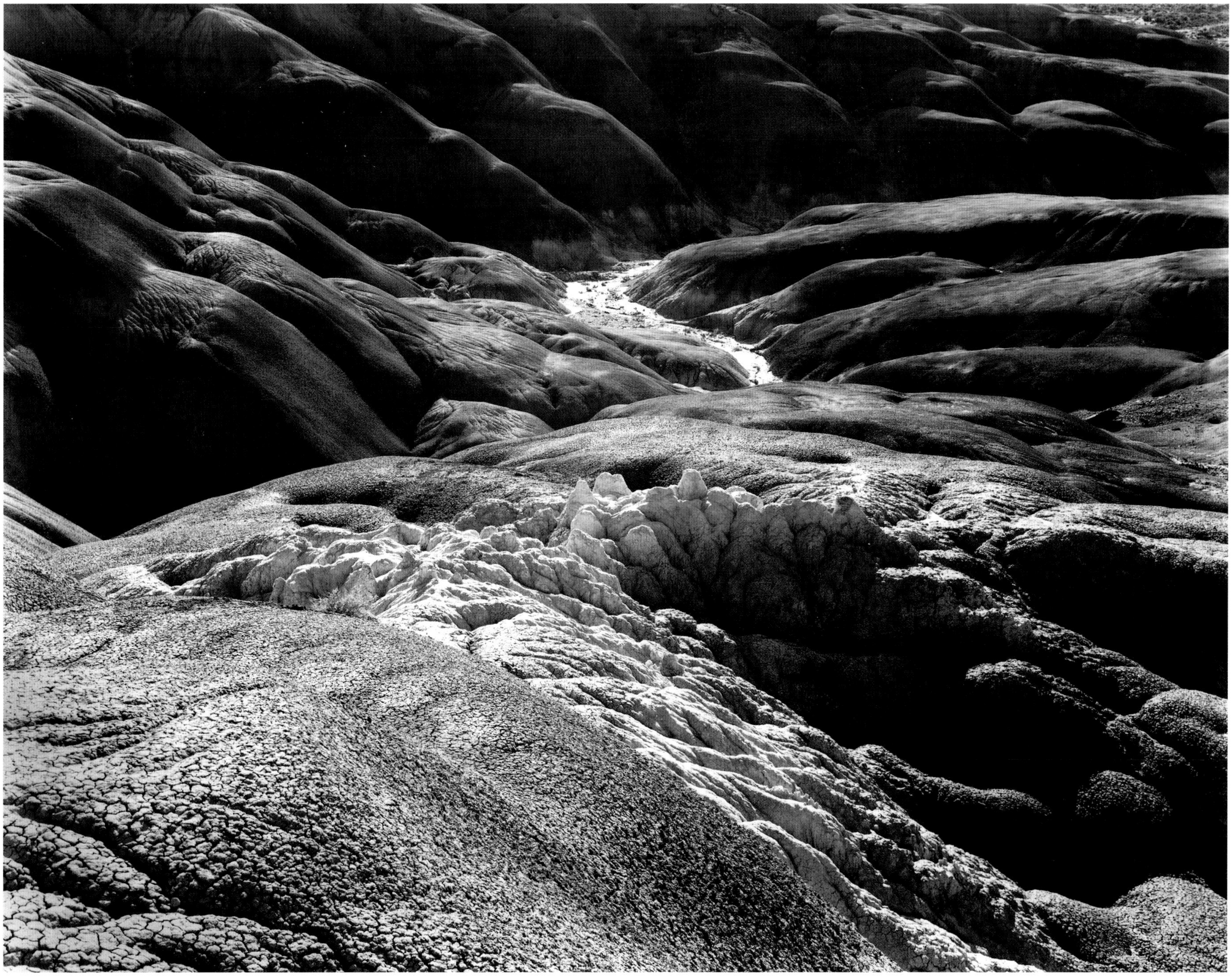

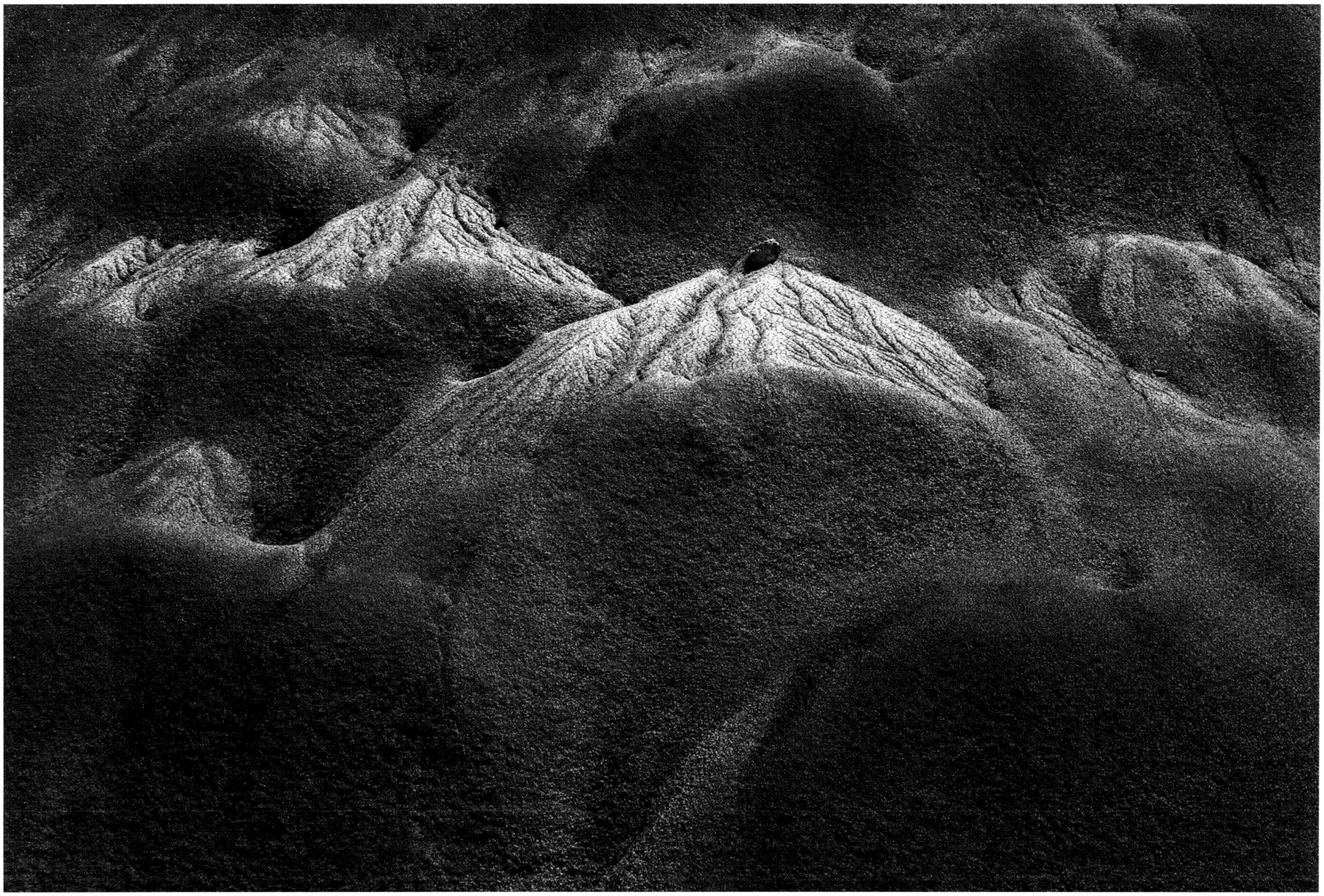

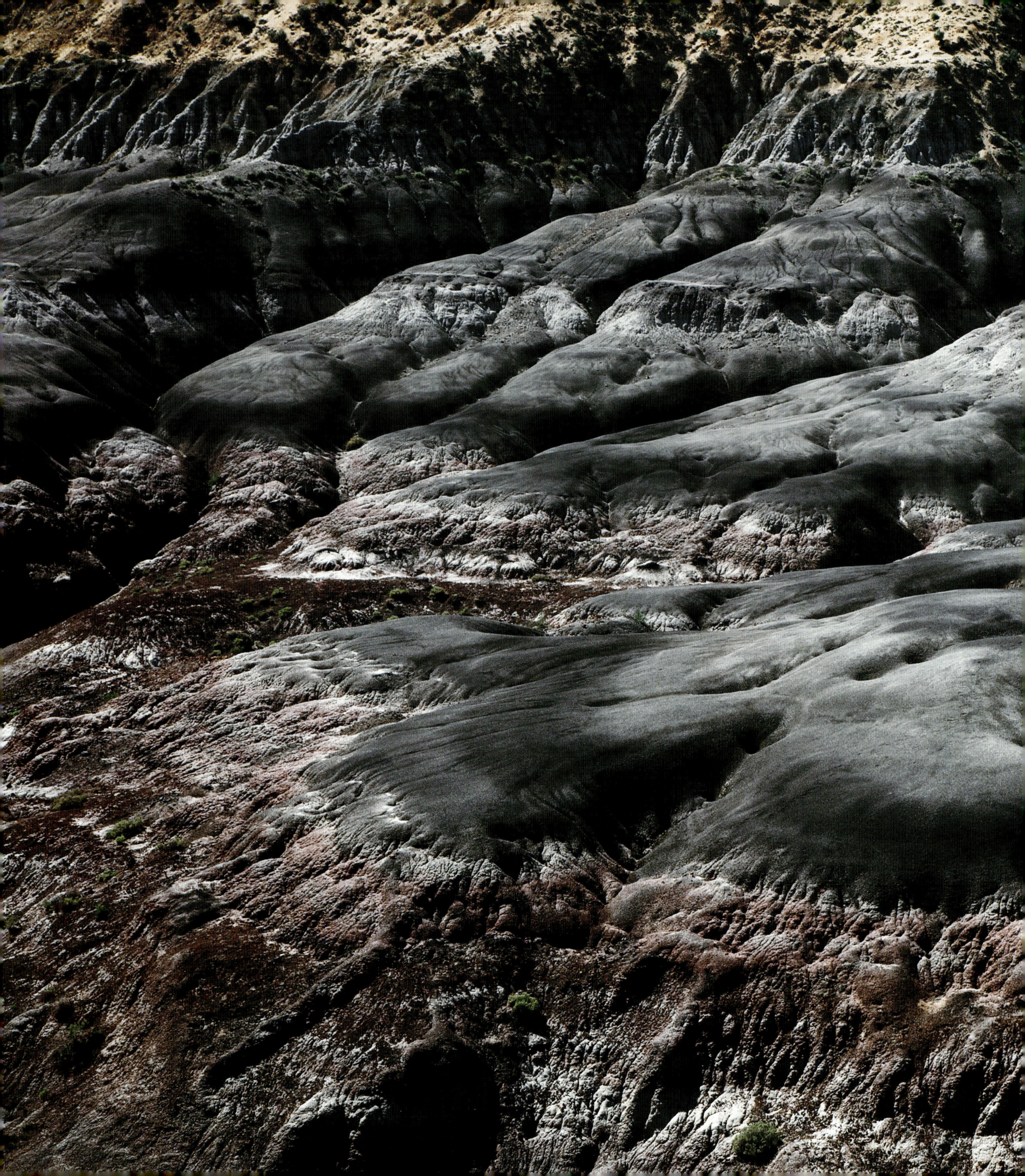

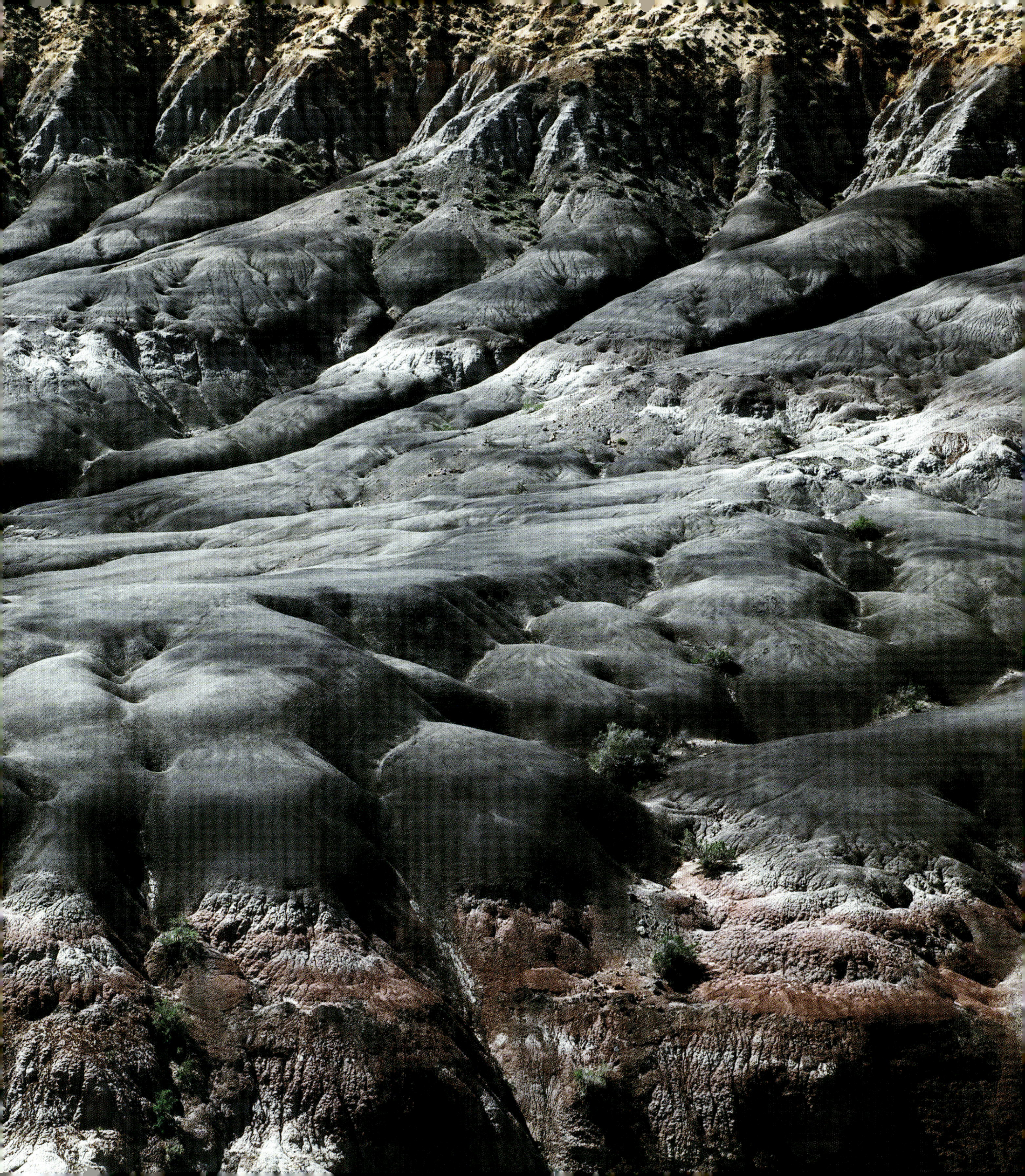

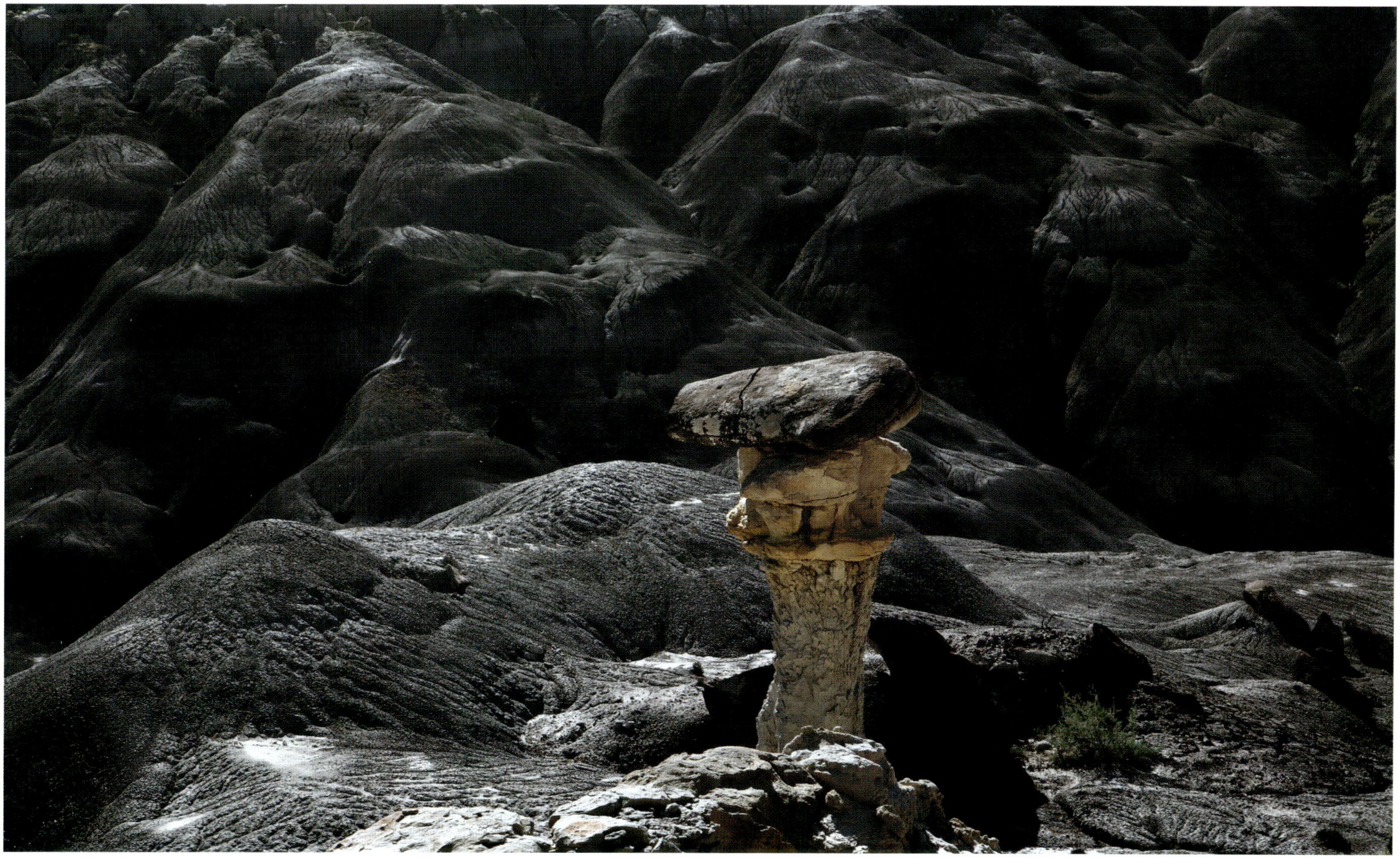

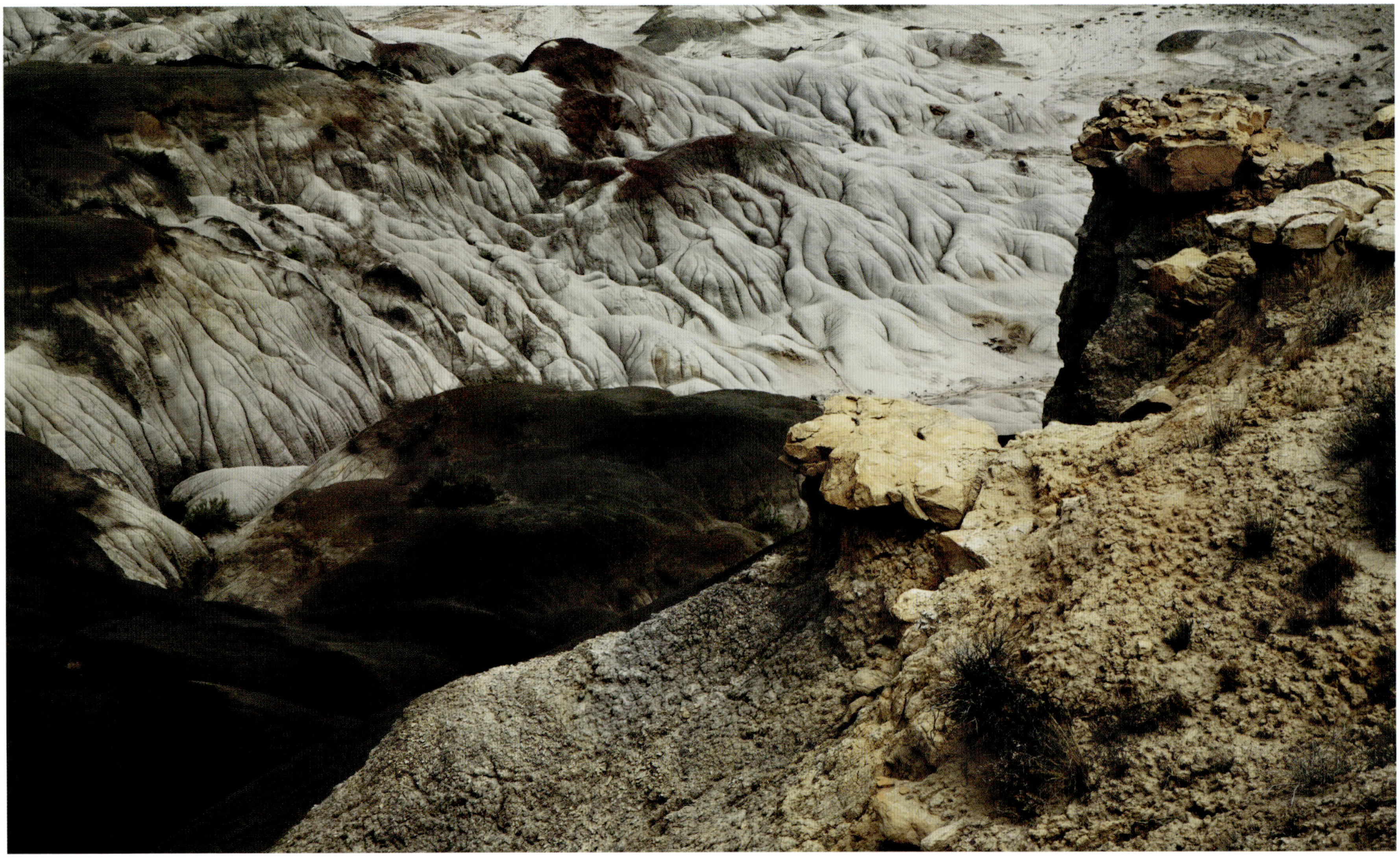

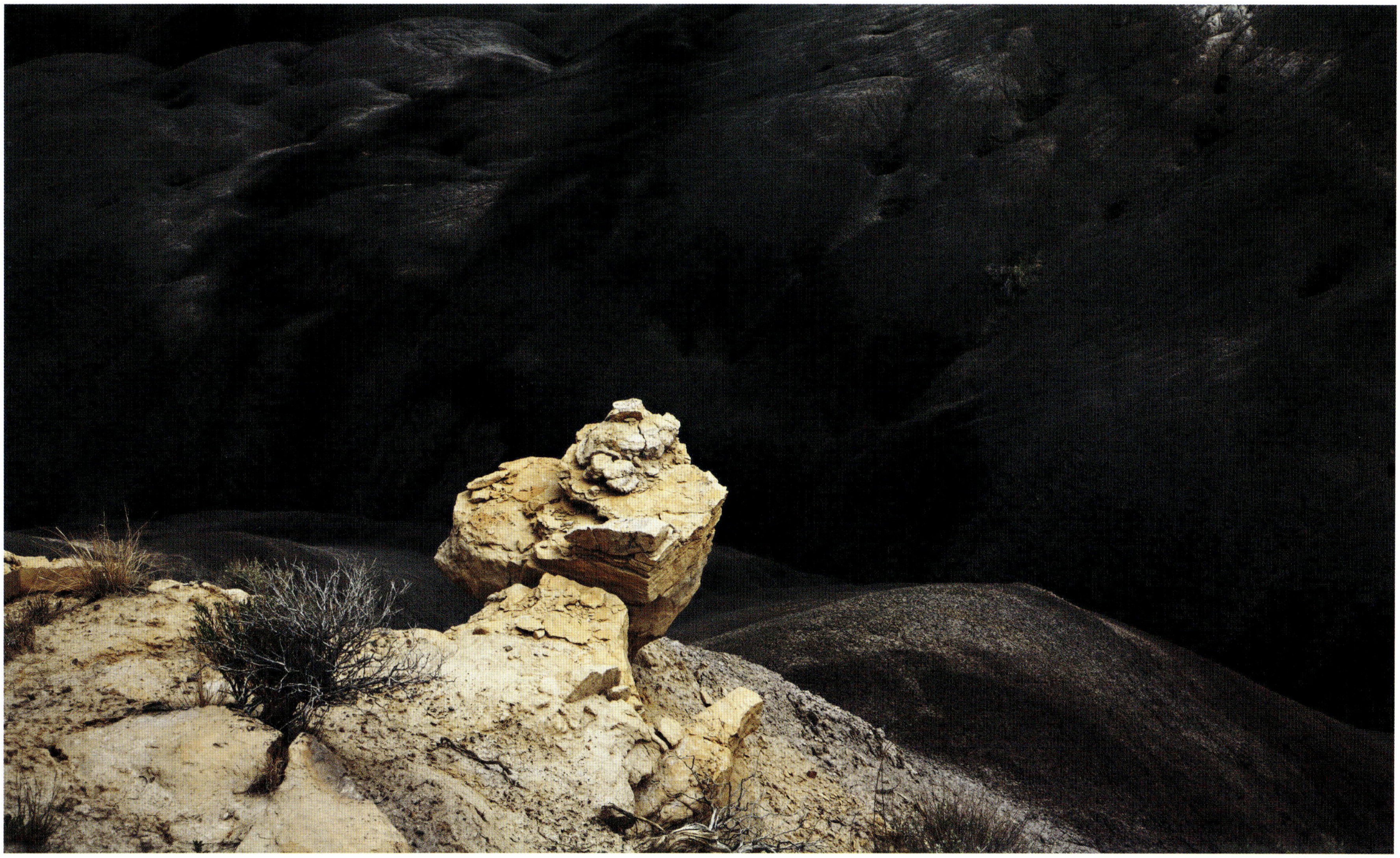

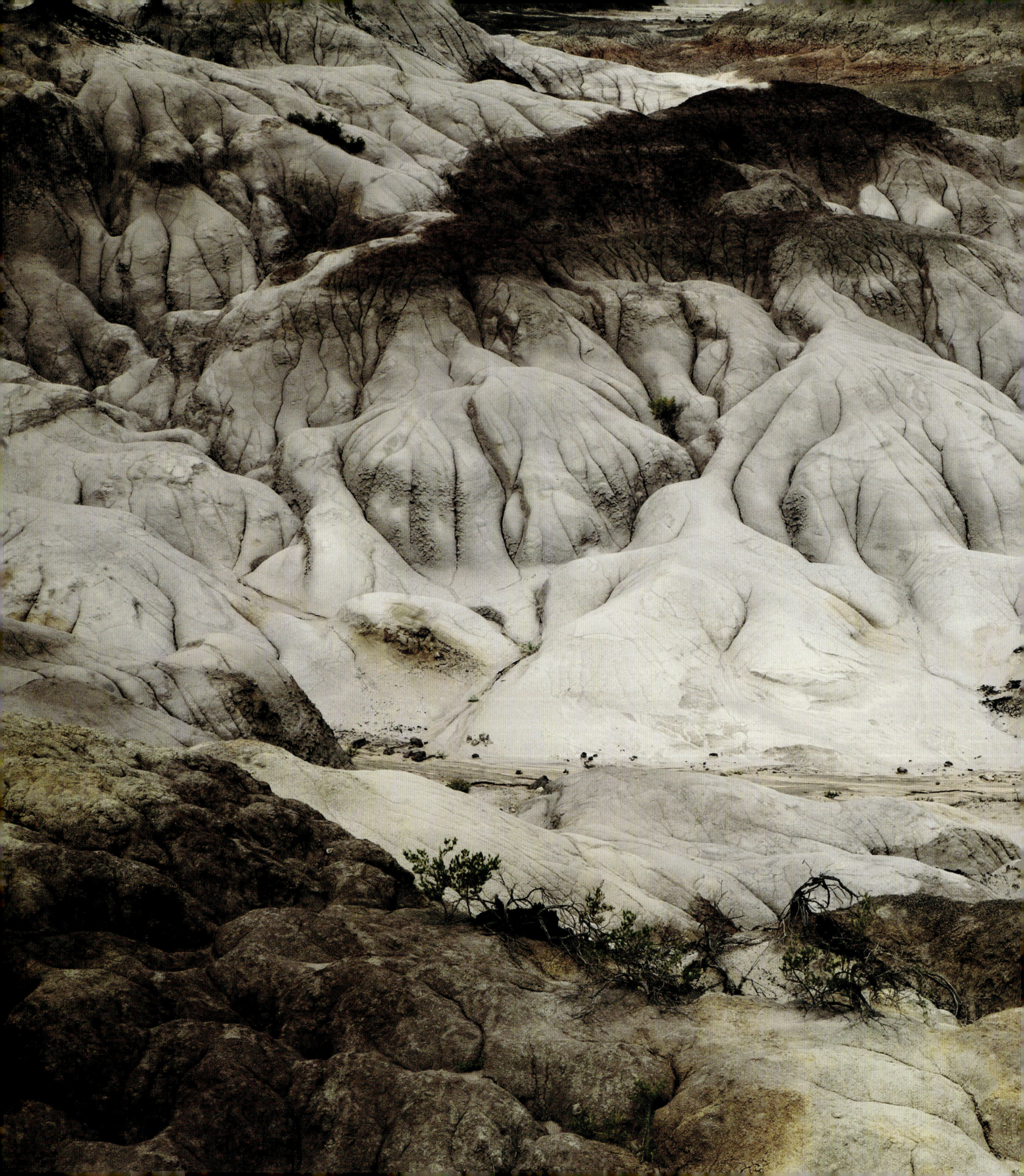

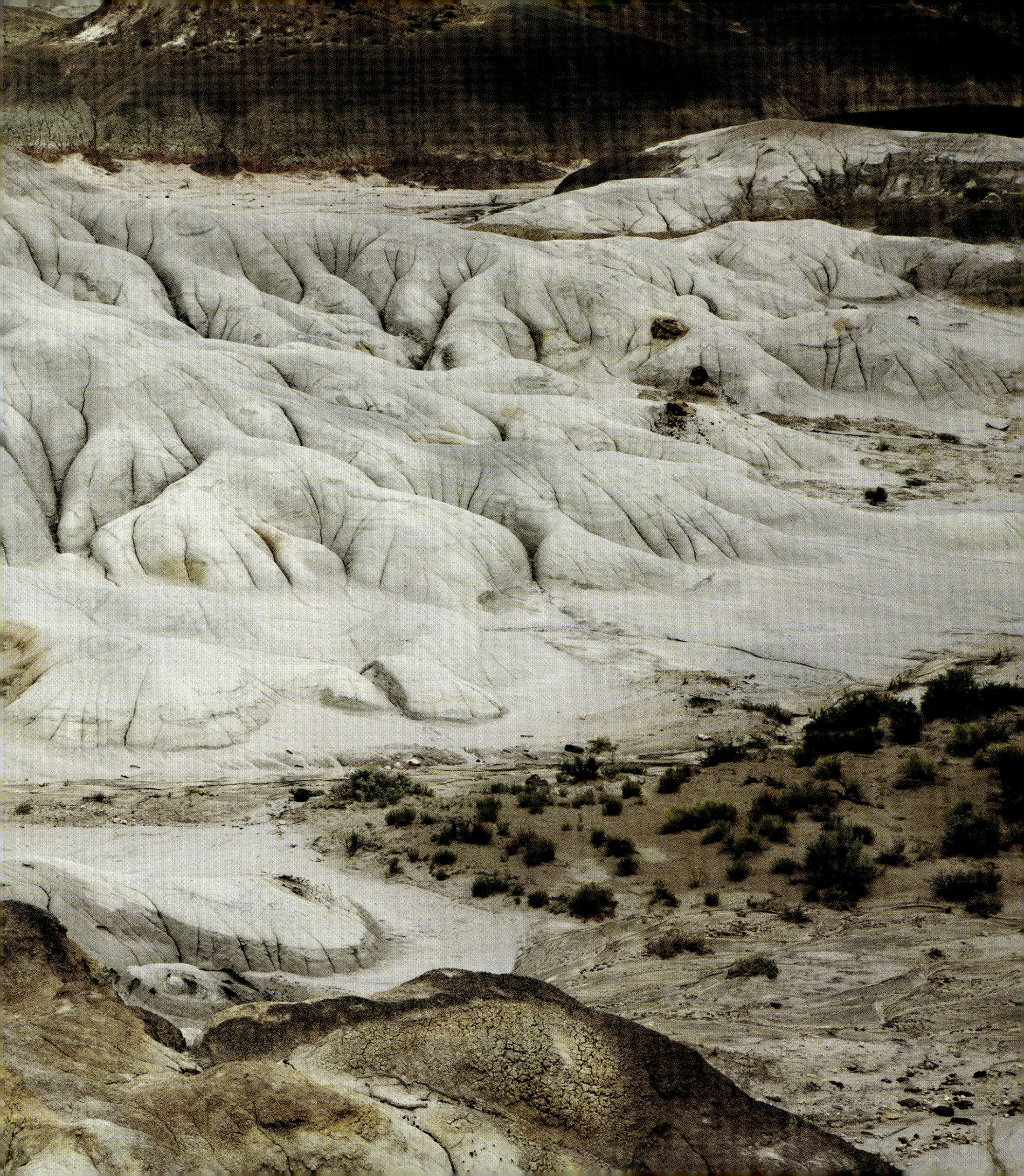

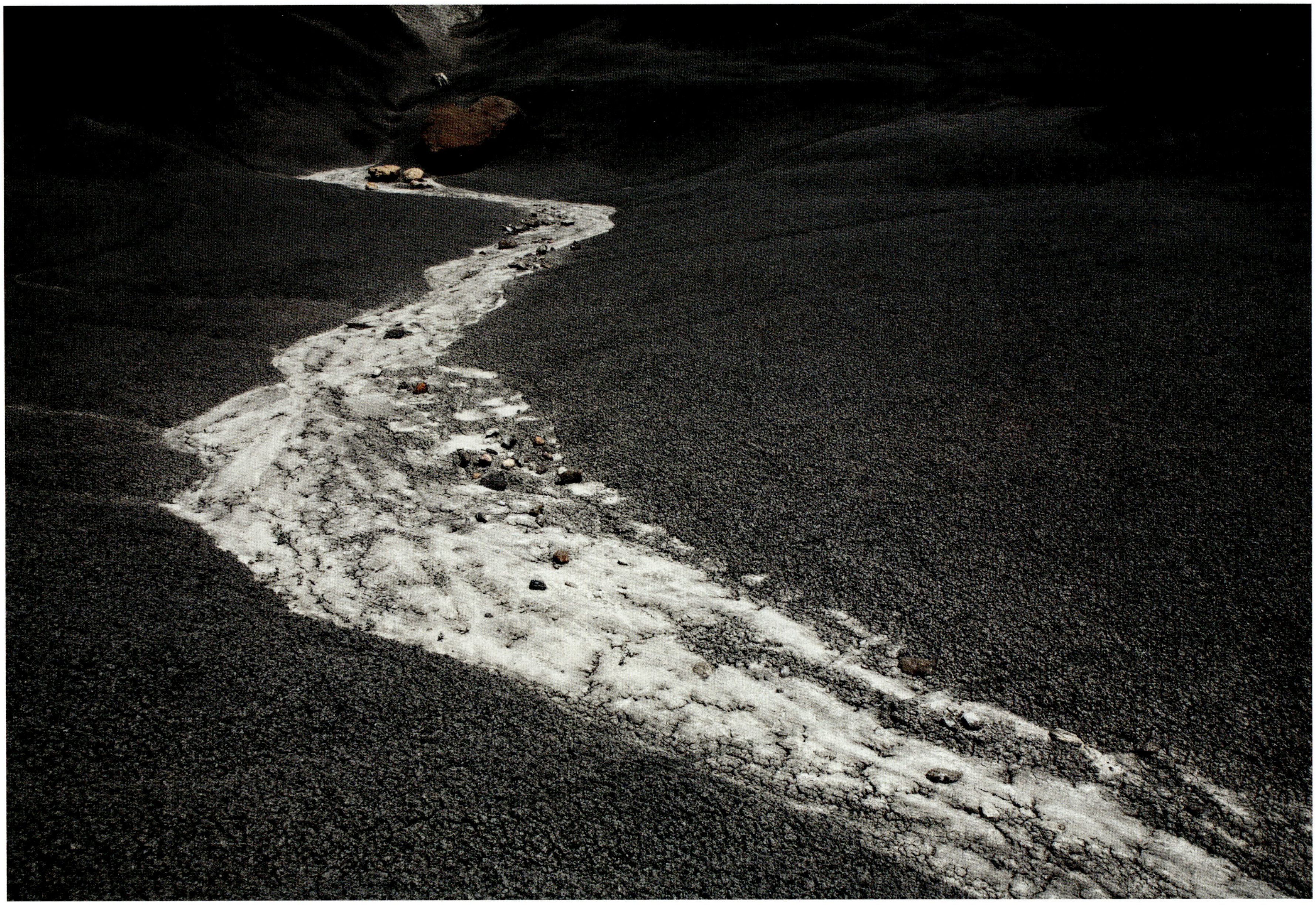

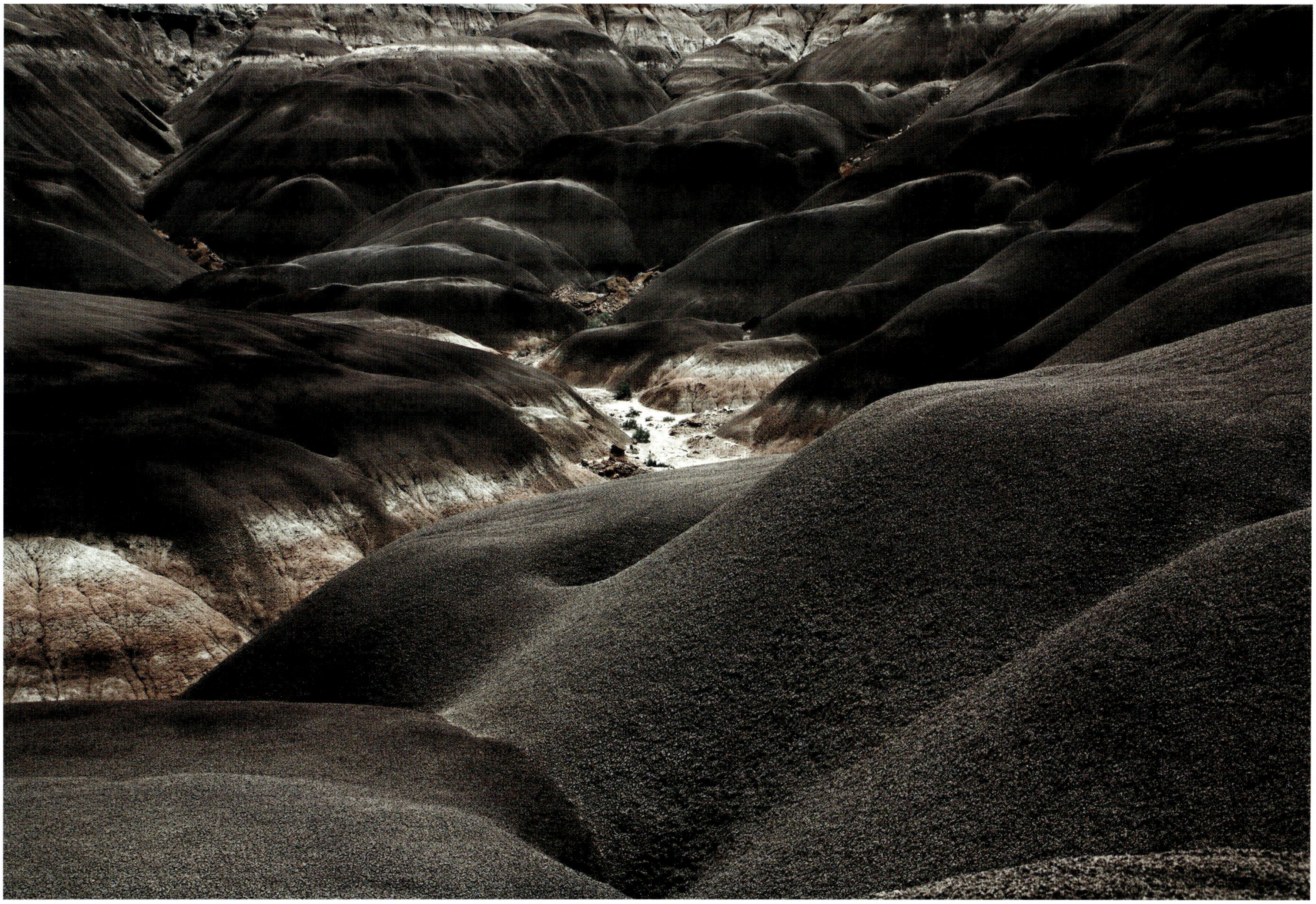

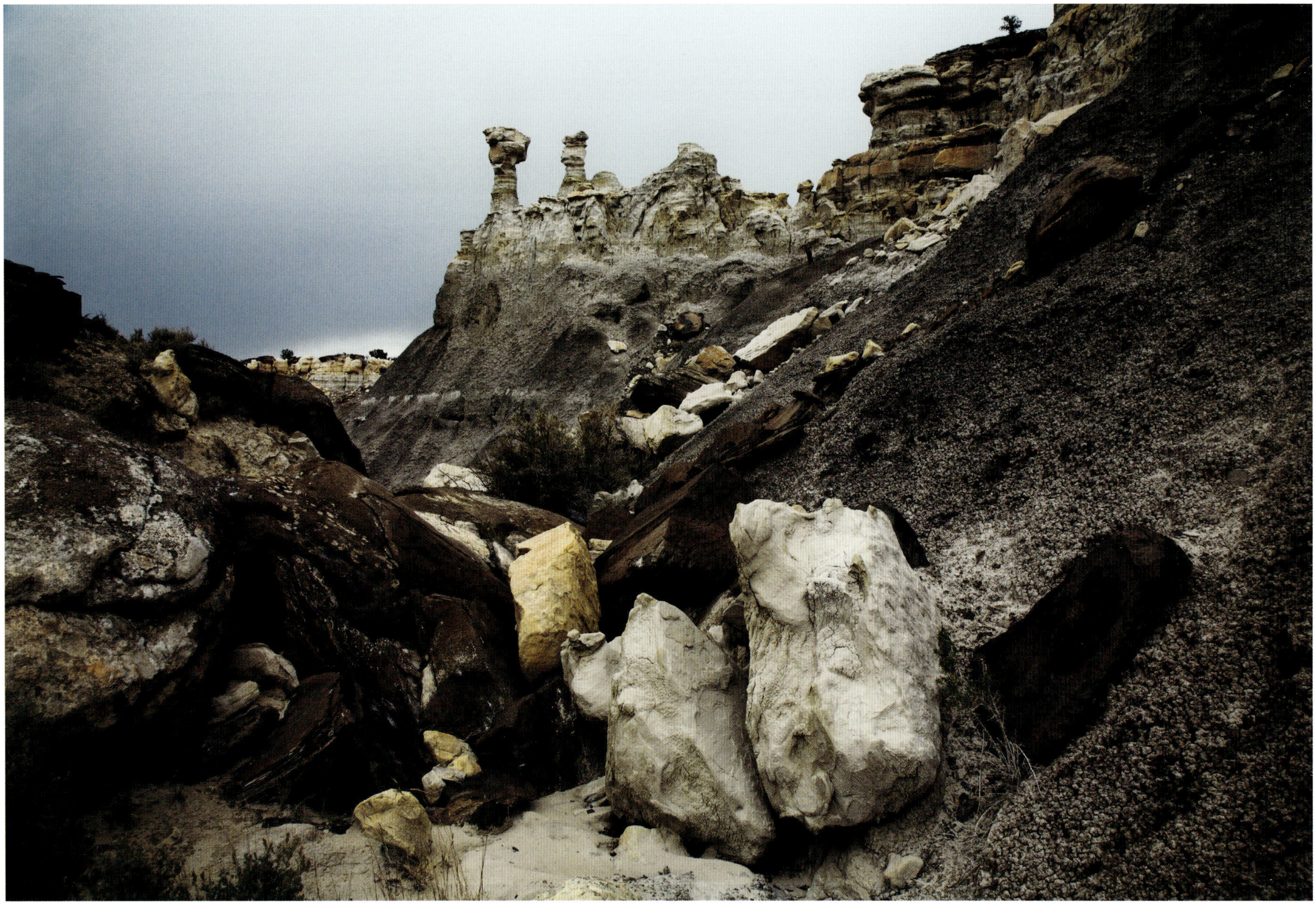

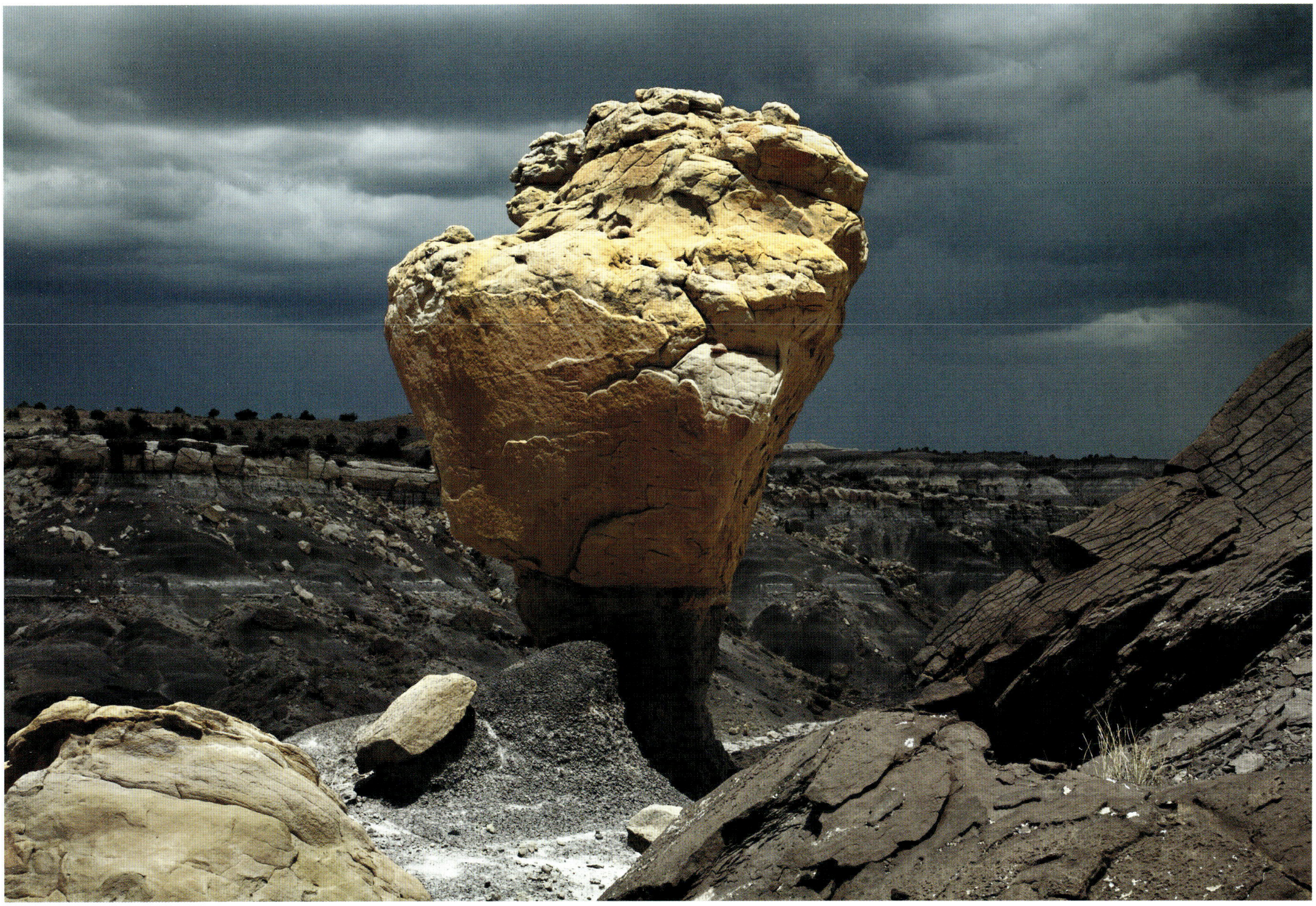

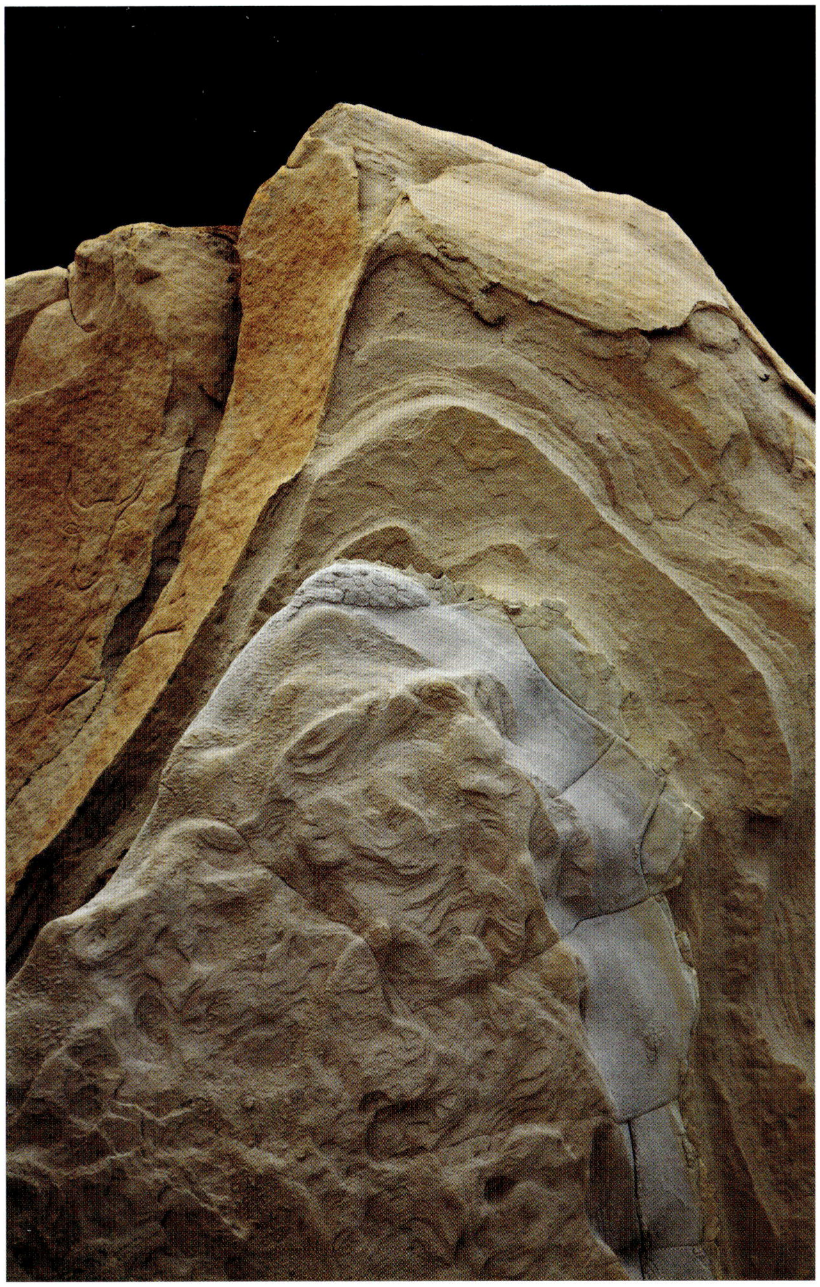

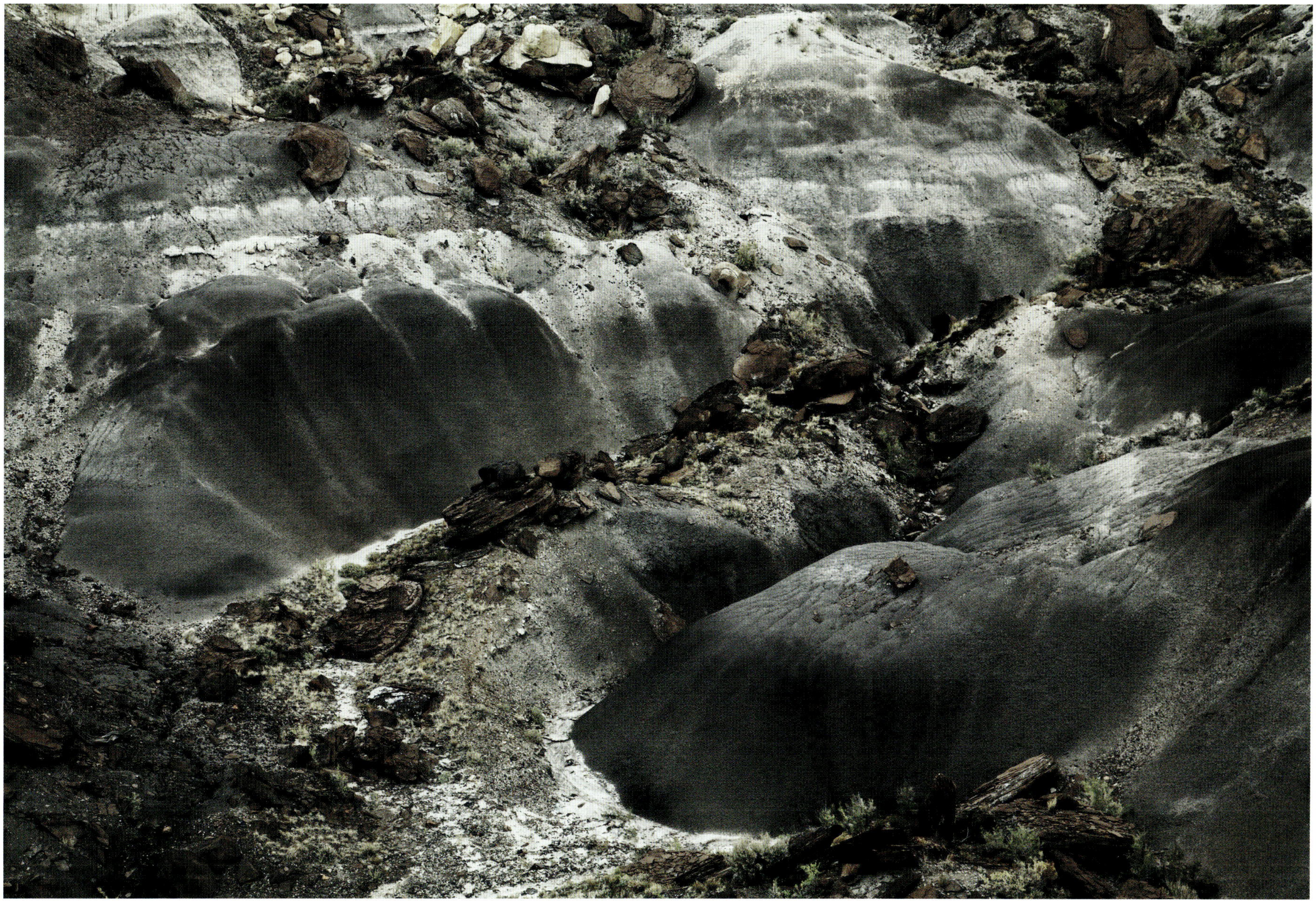

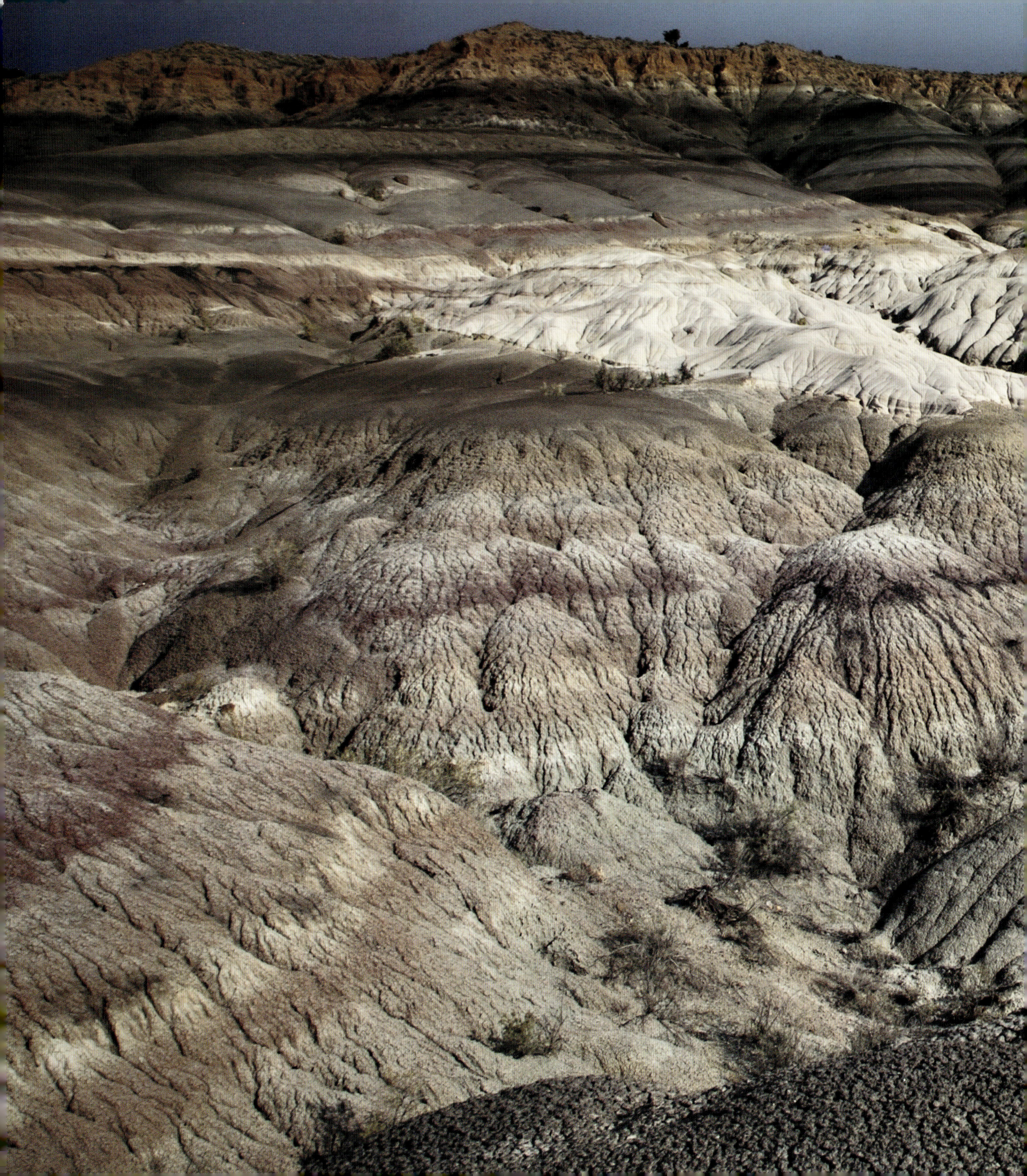

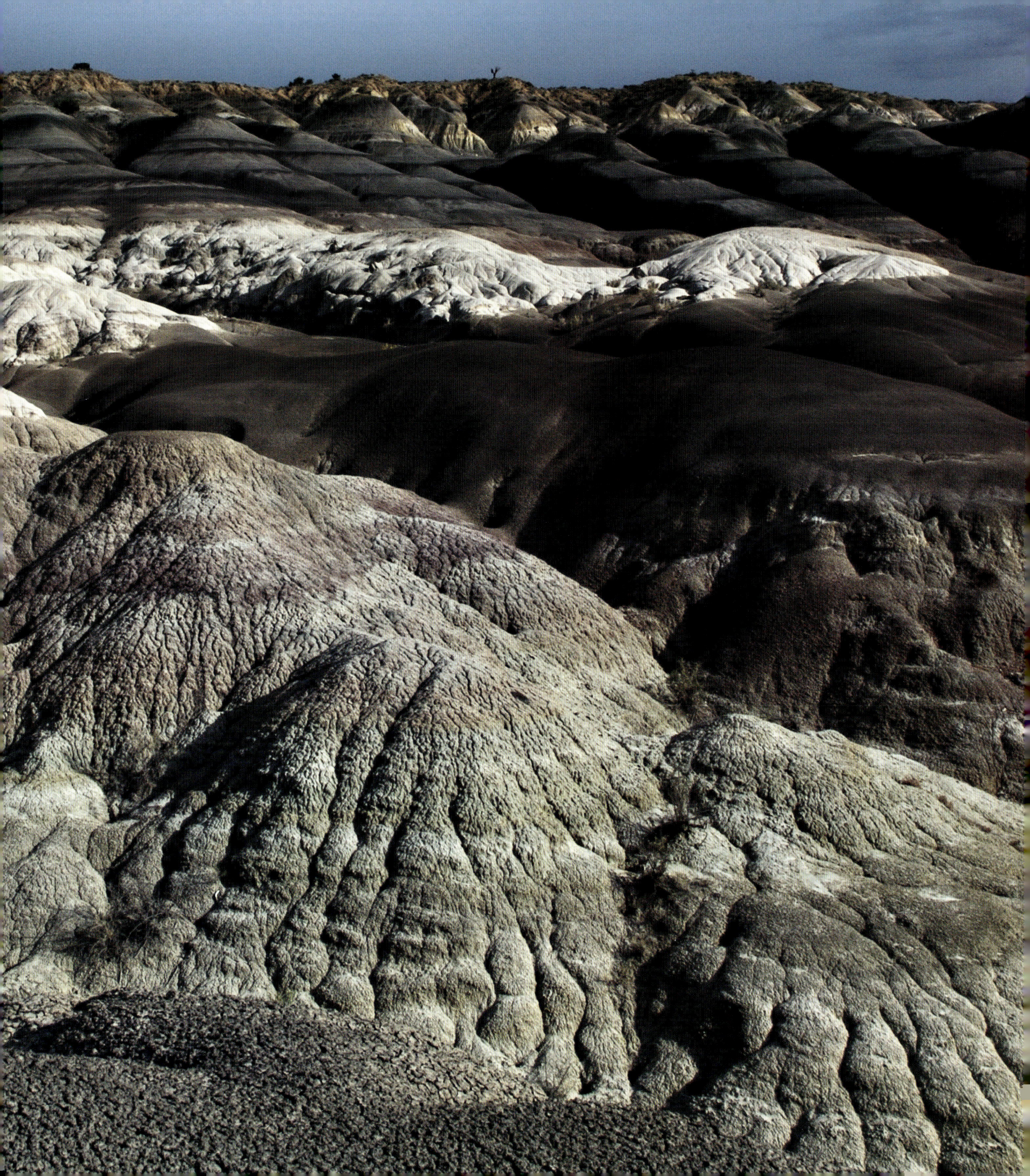

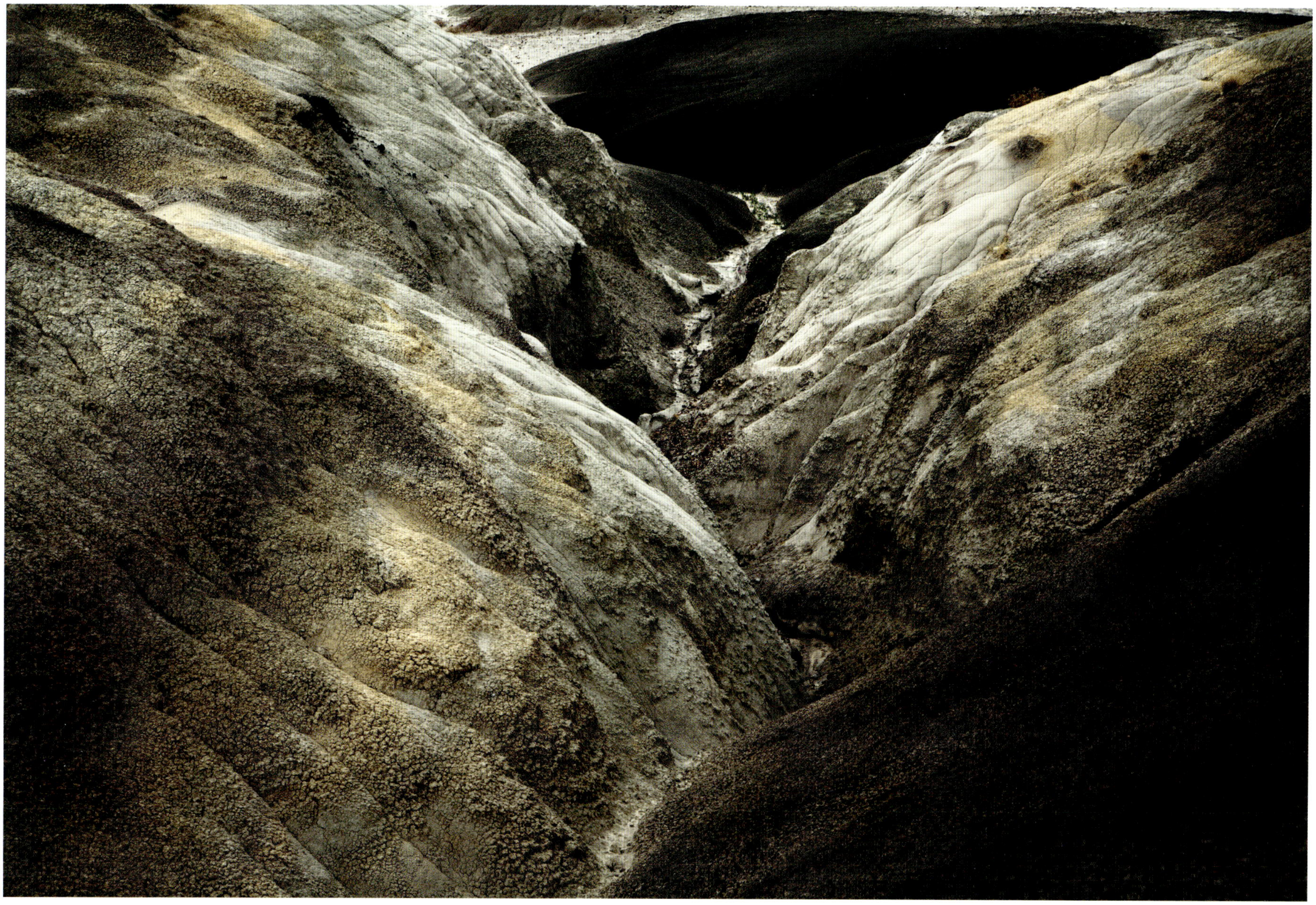

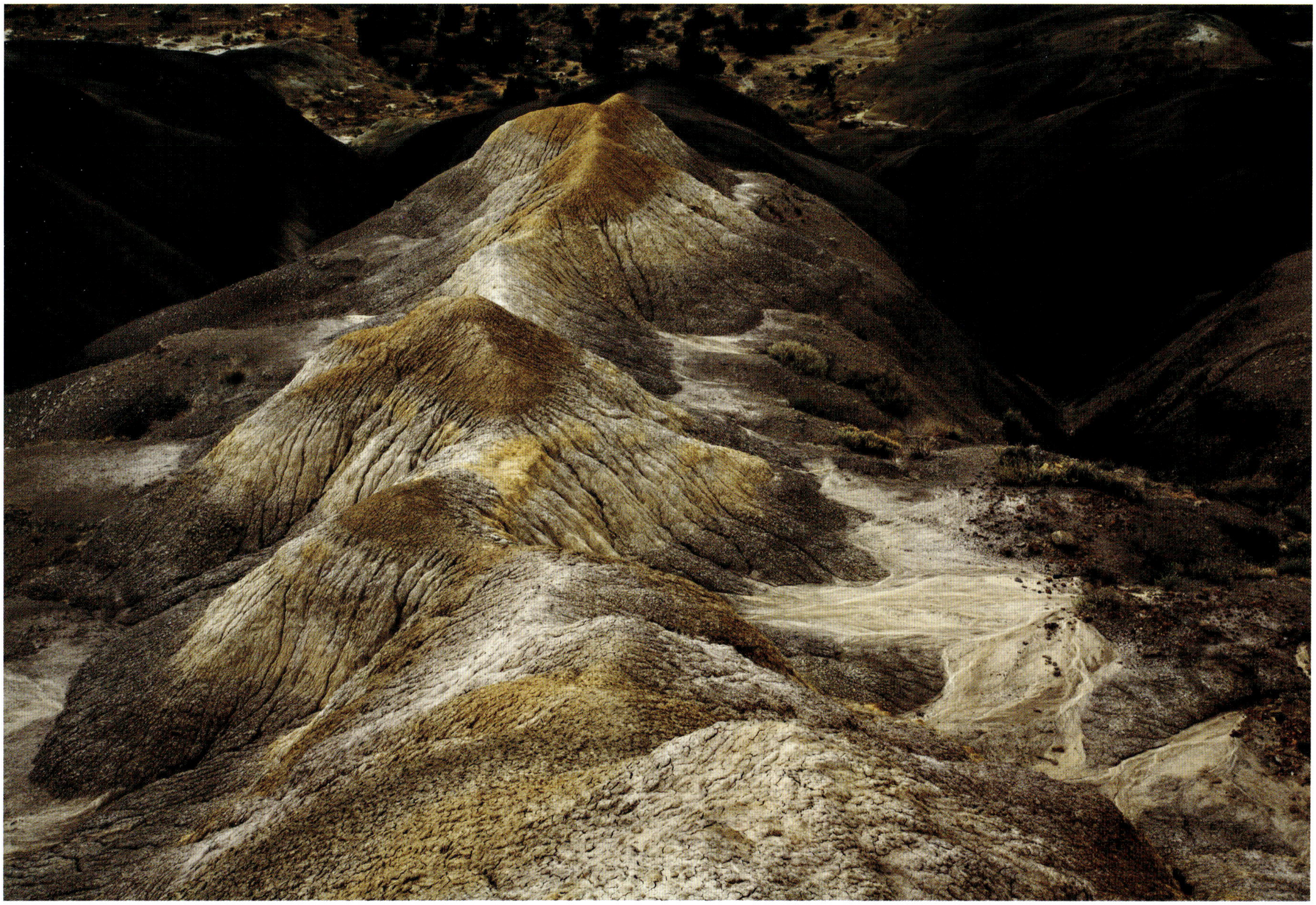

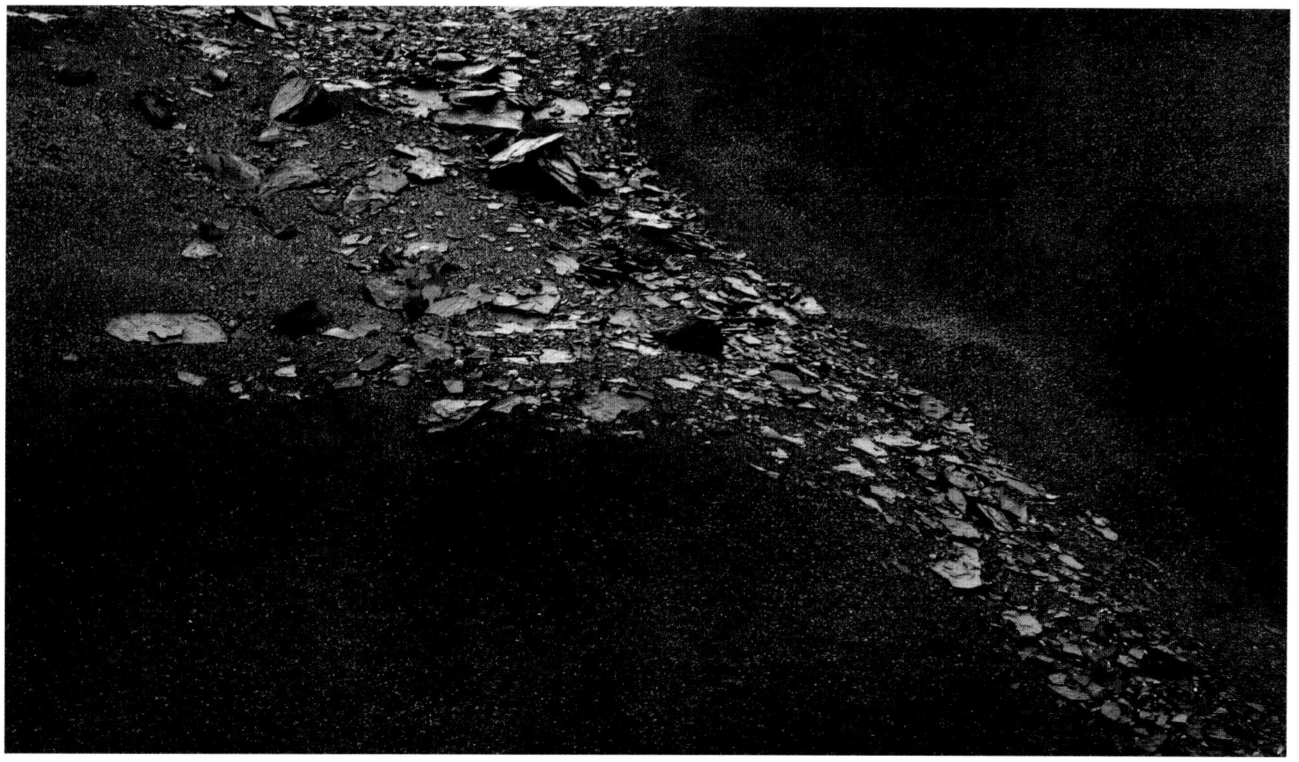

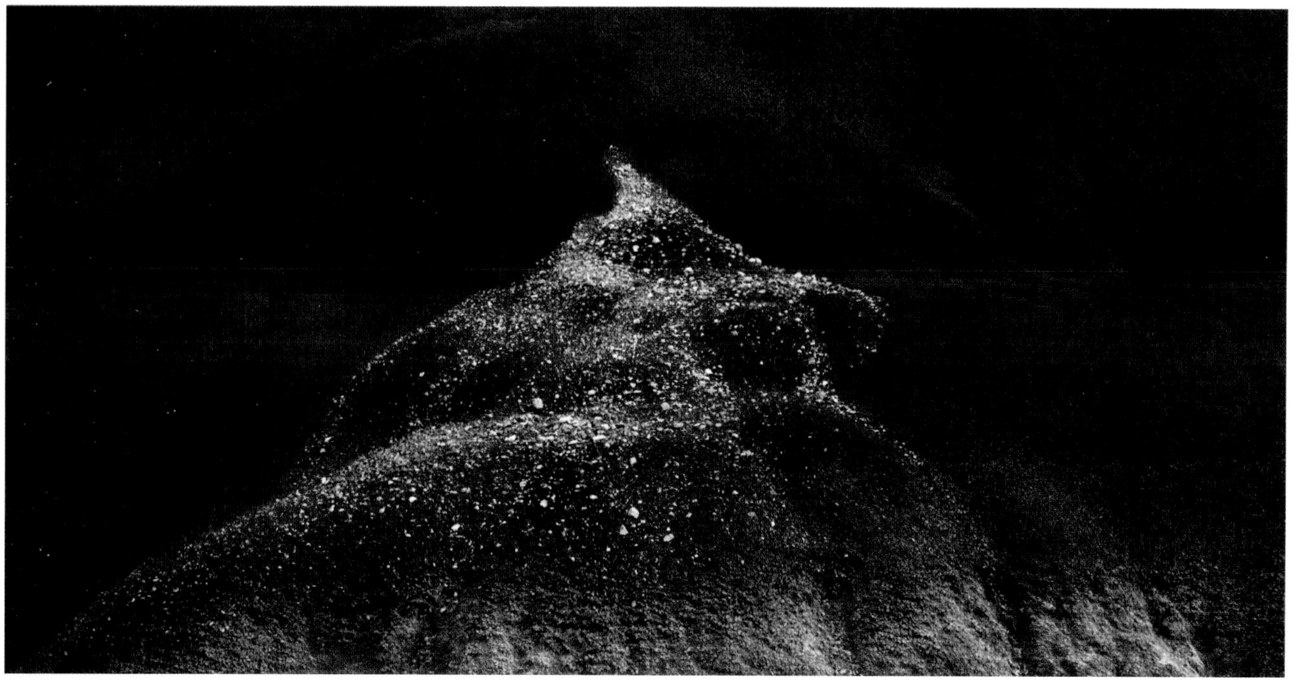

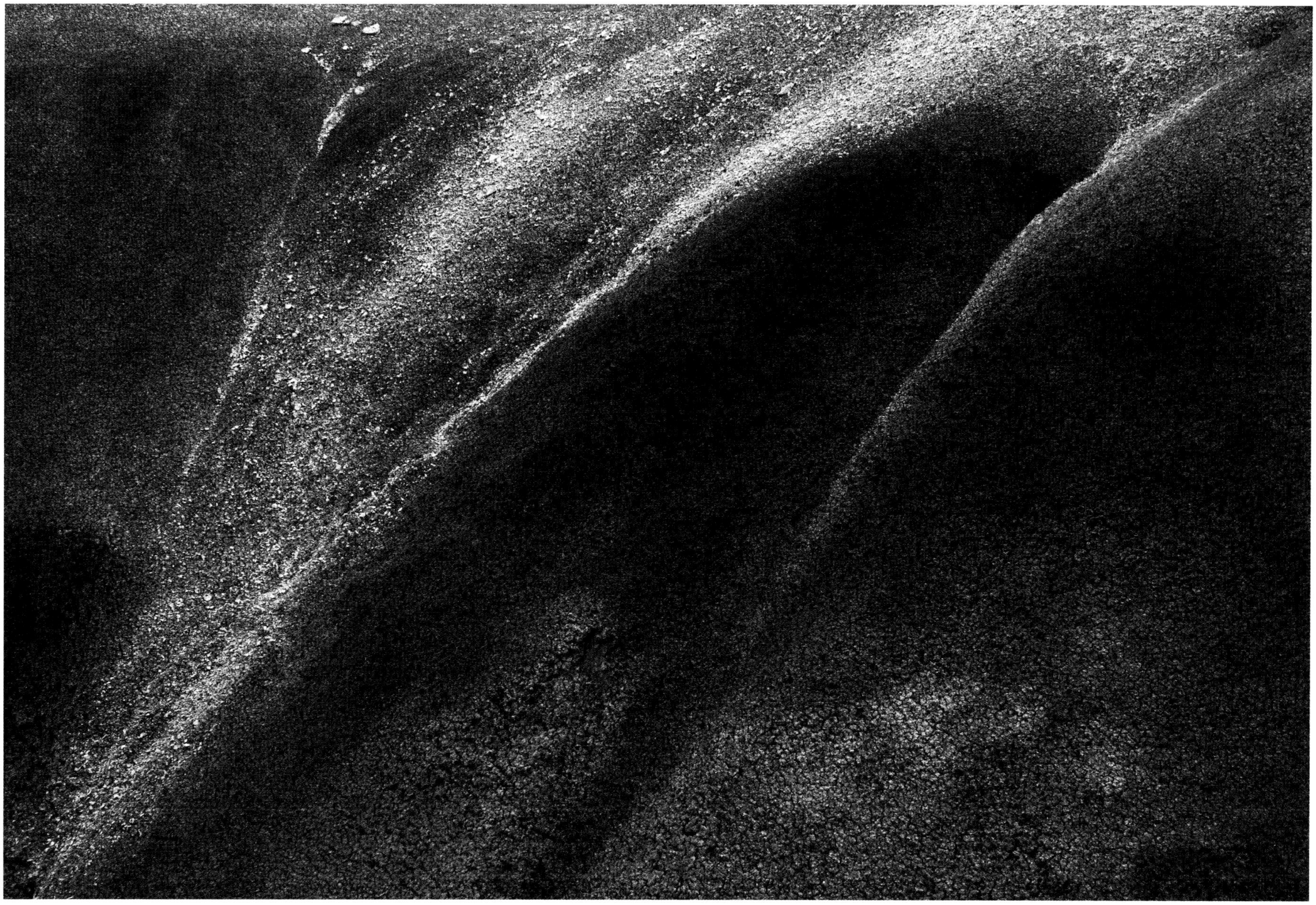

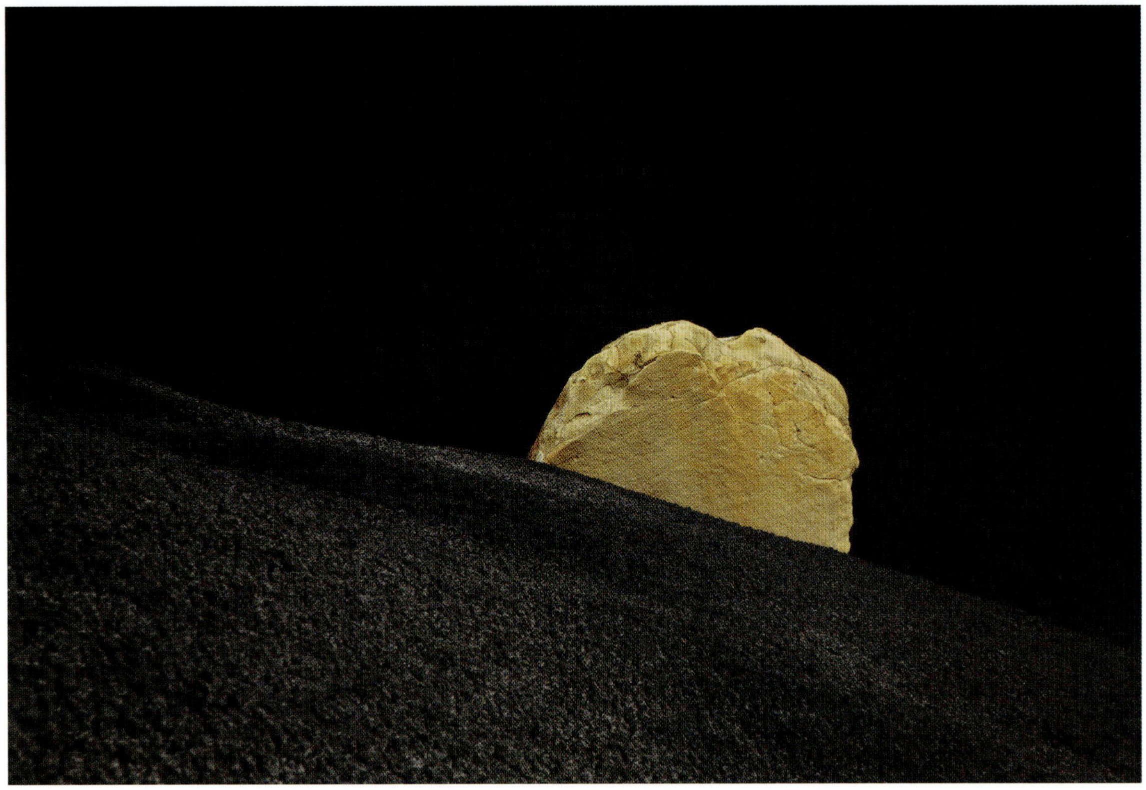

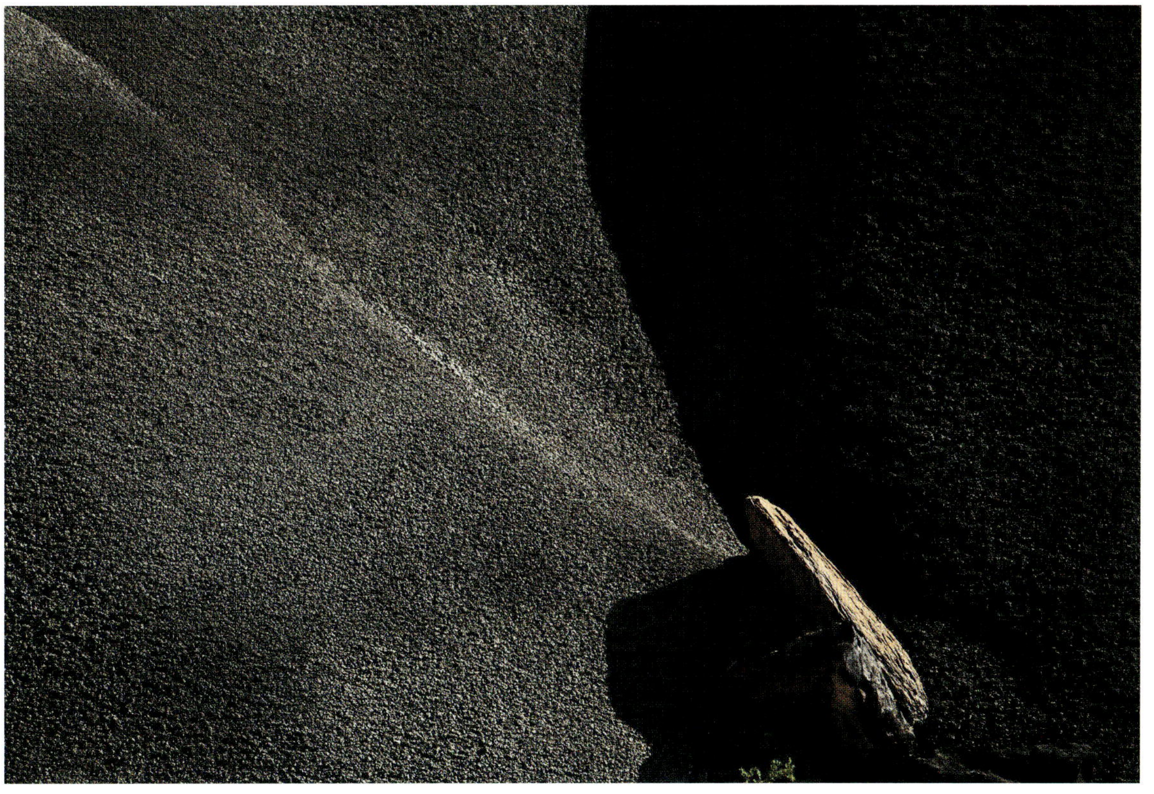

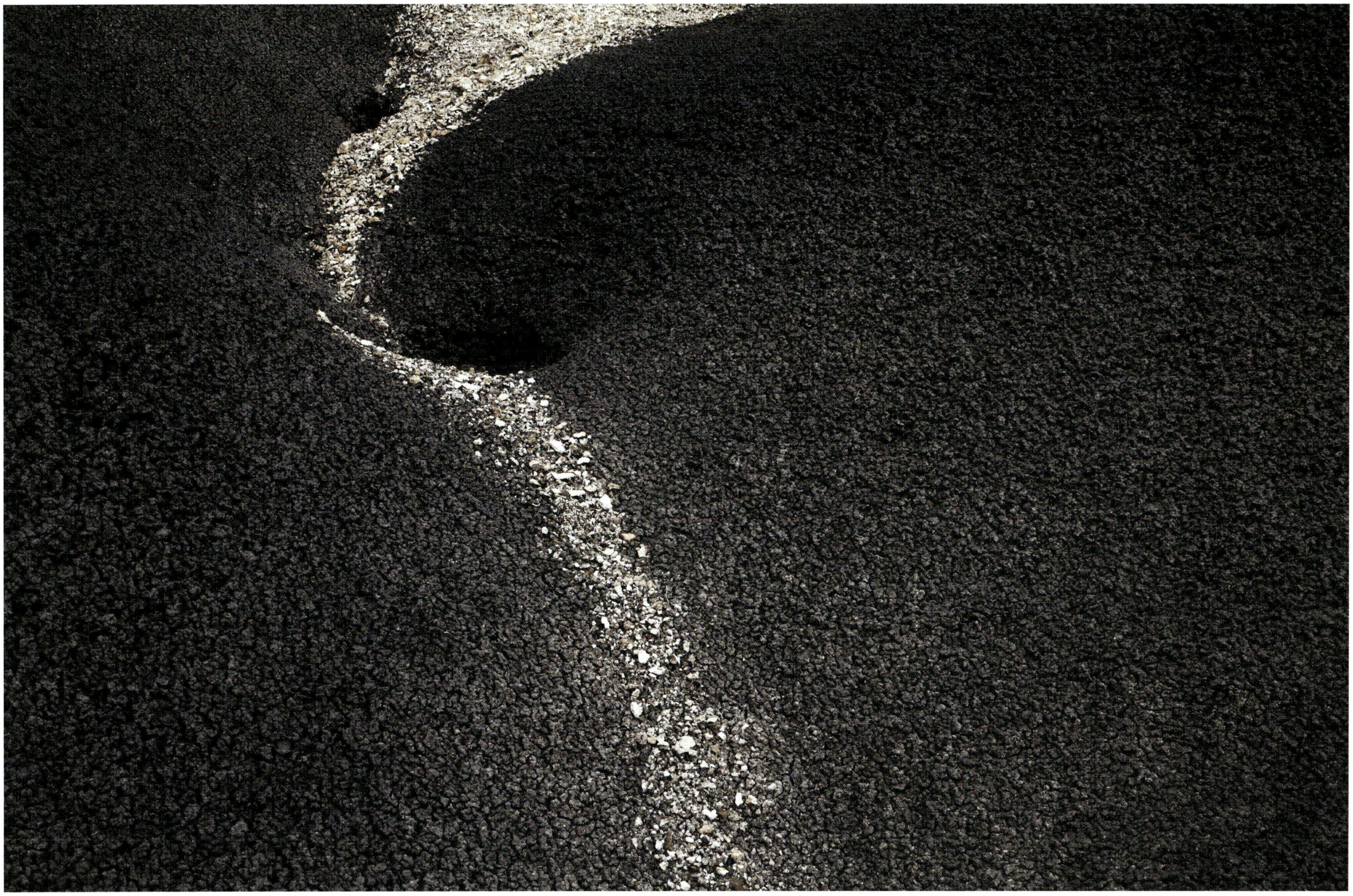

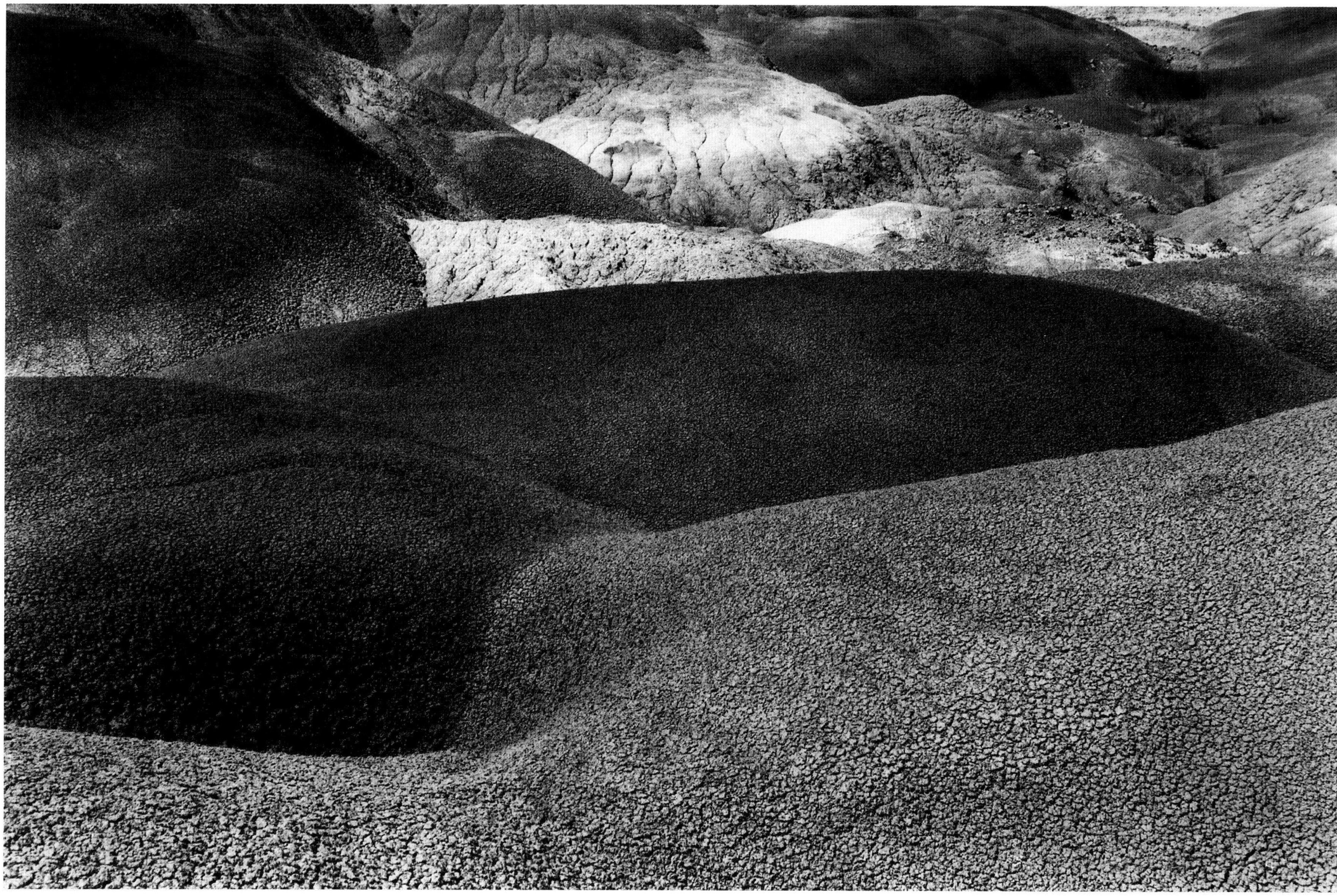

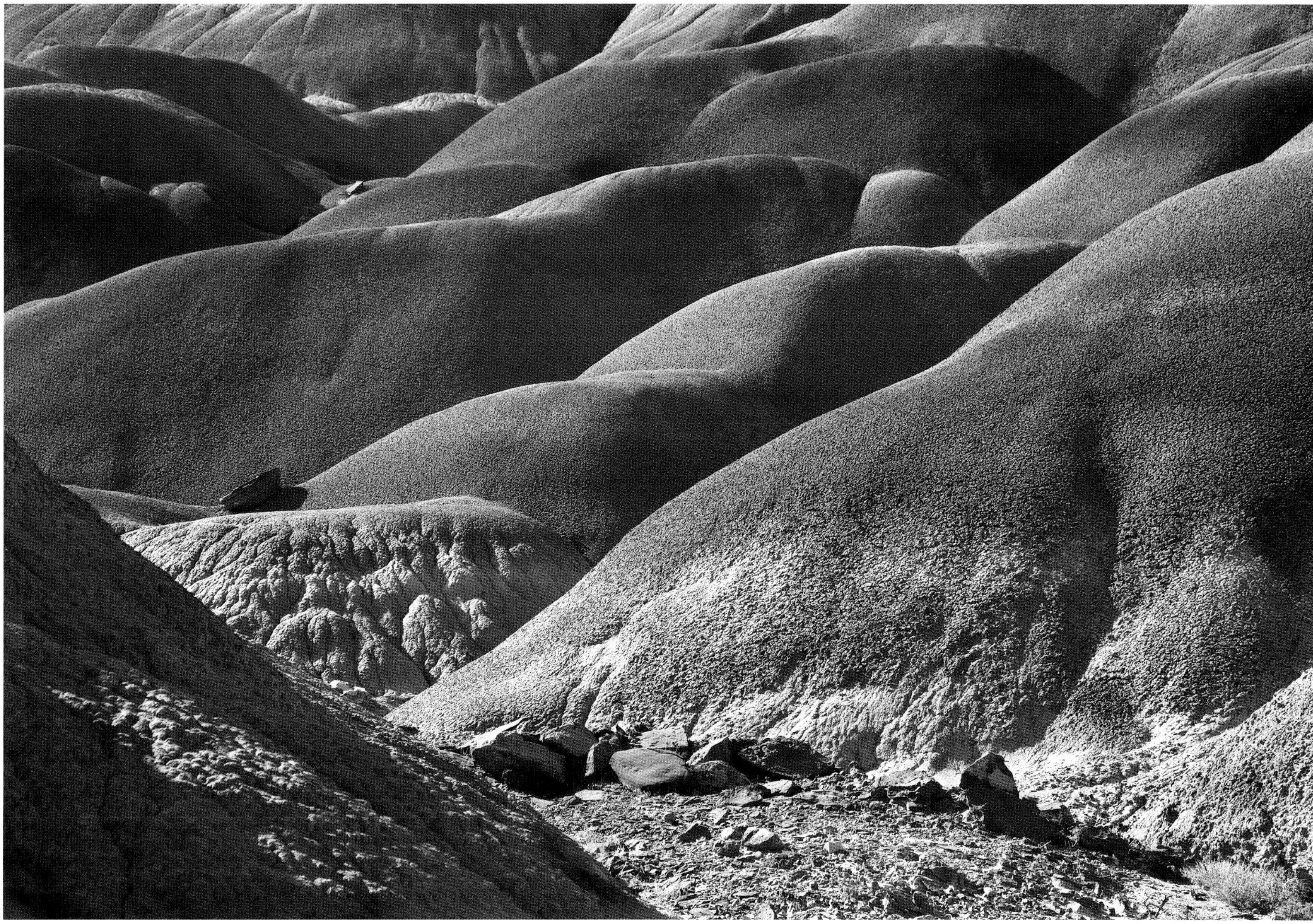

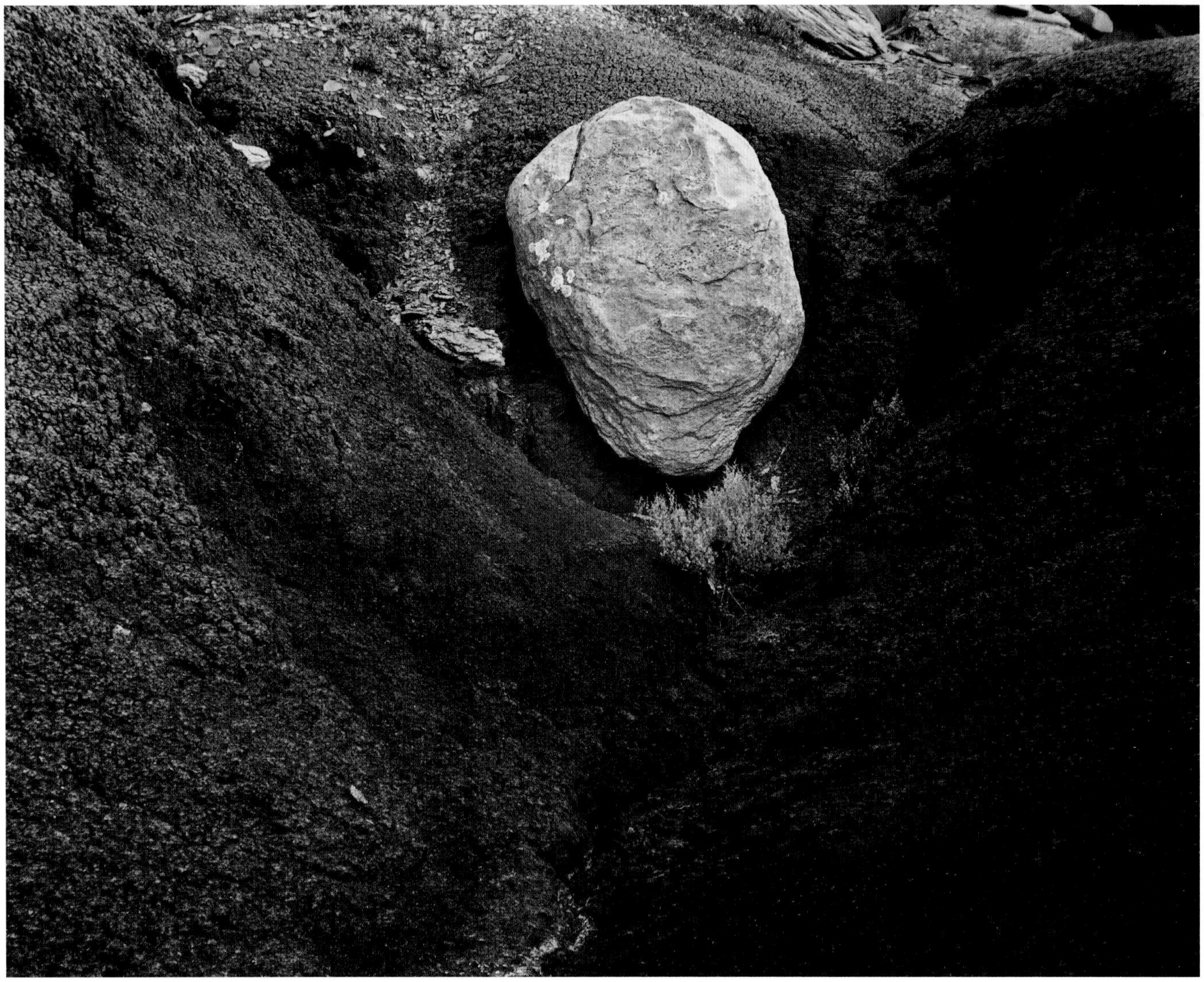

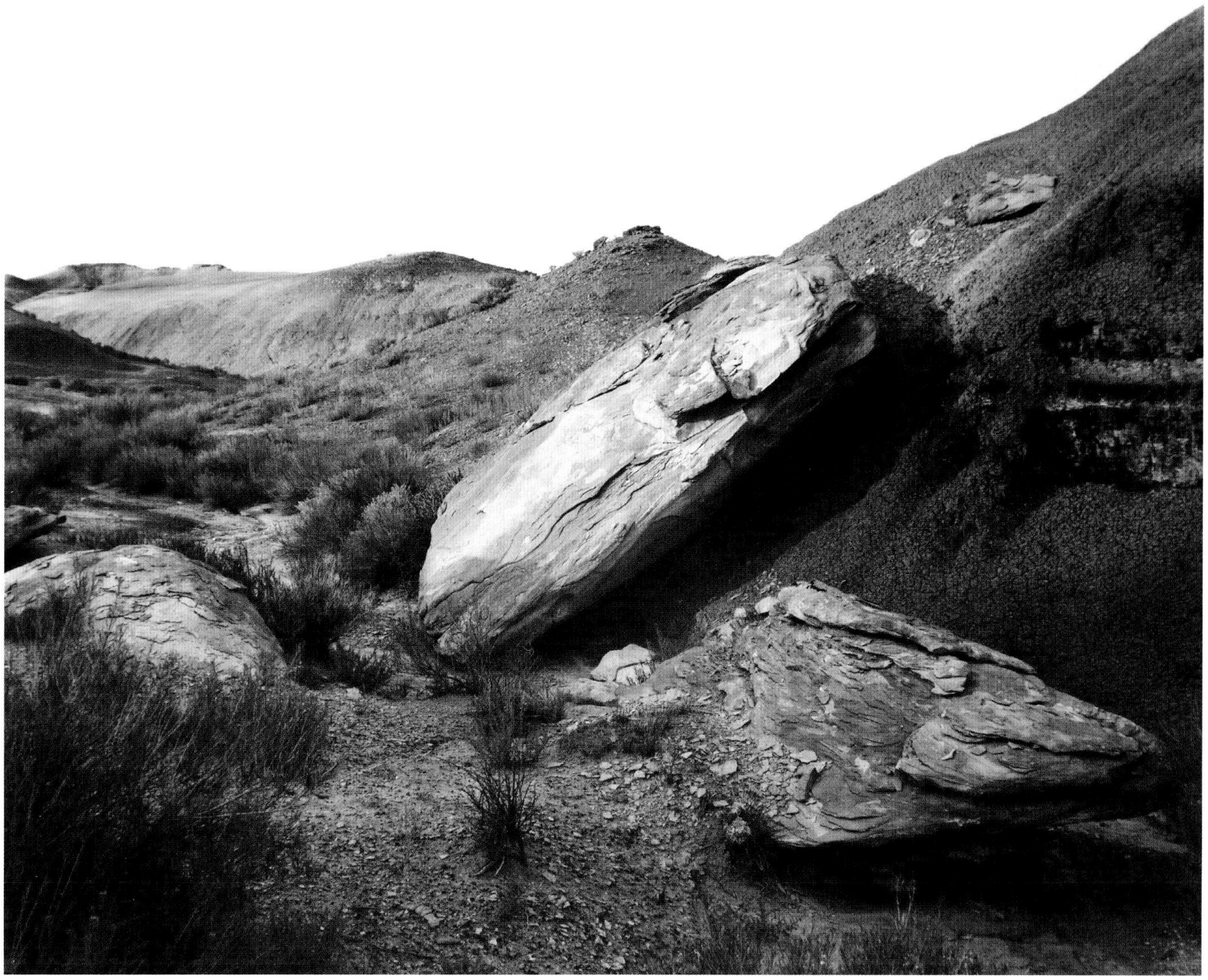

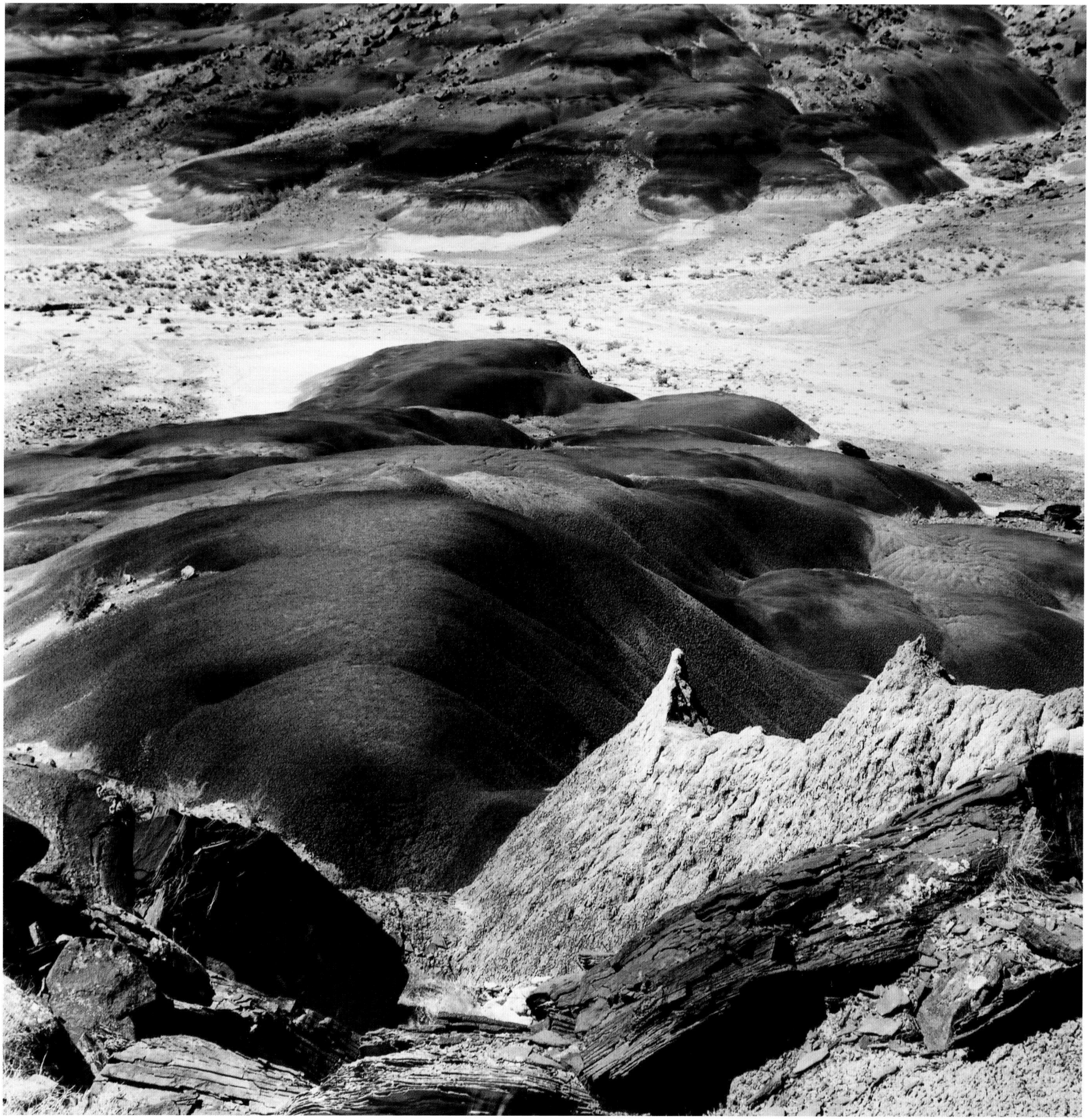

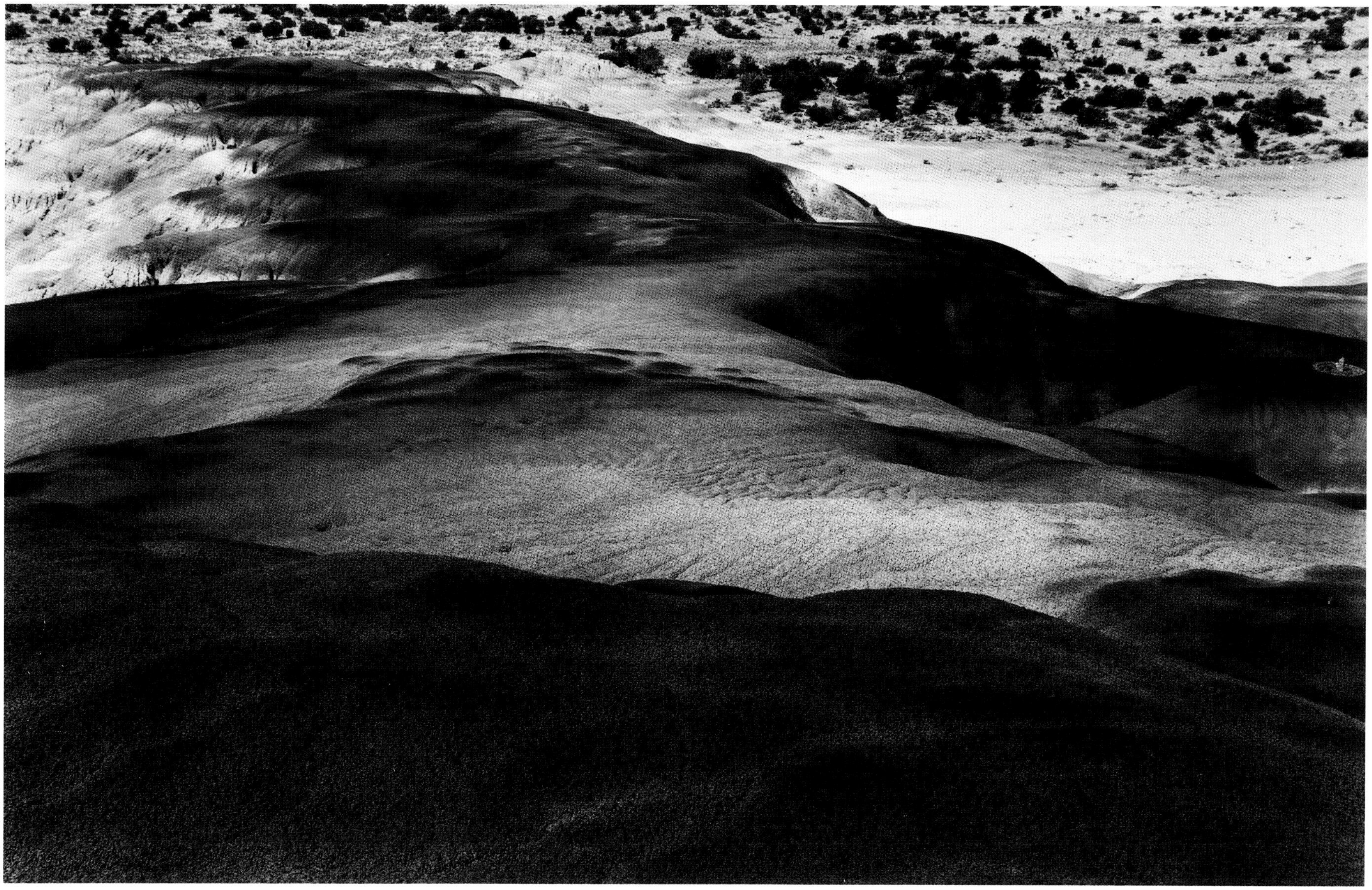

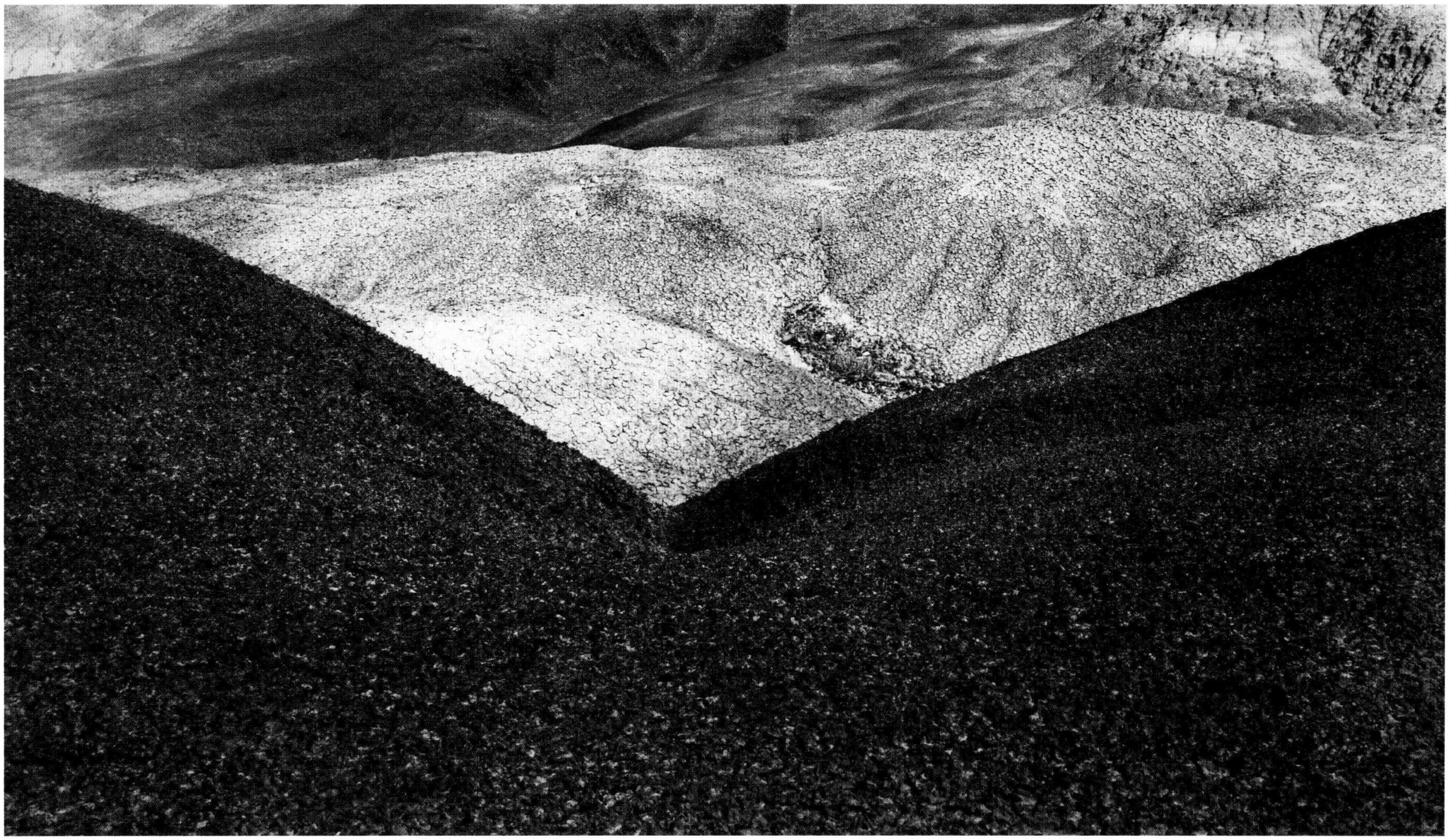

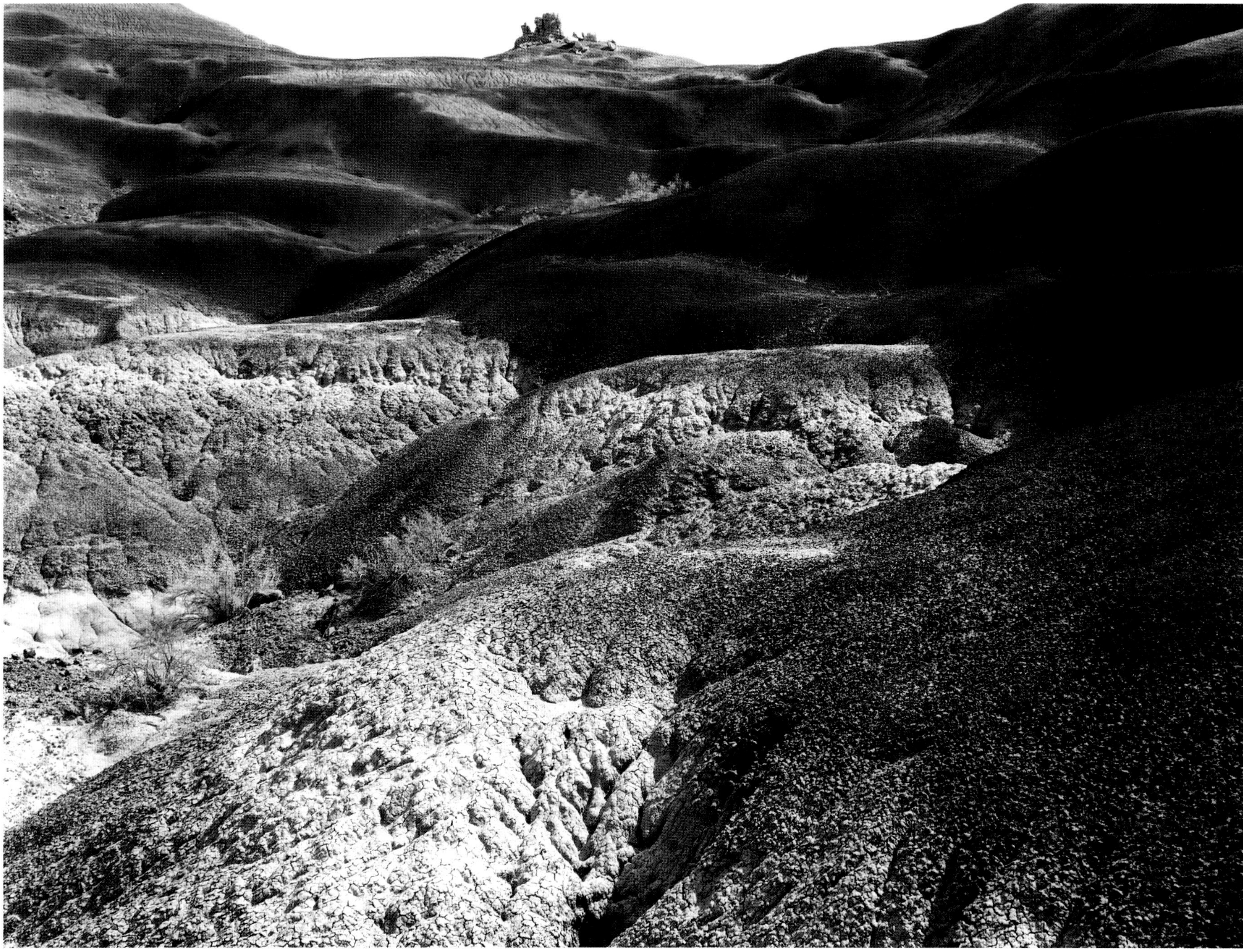

WINTER

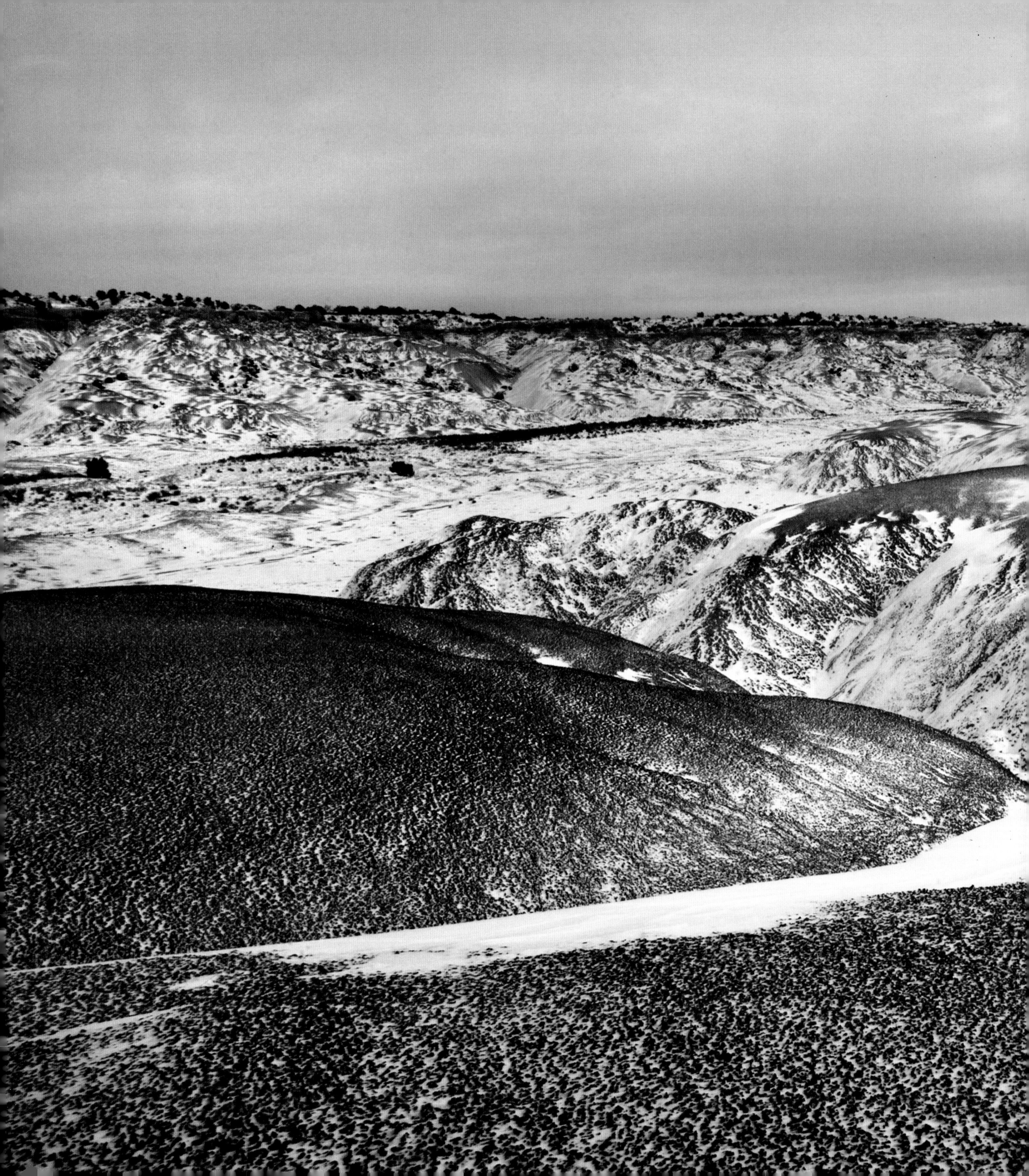

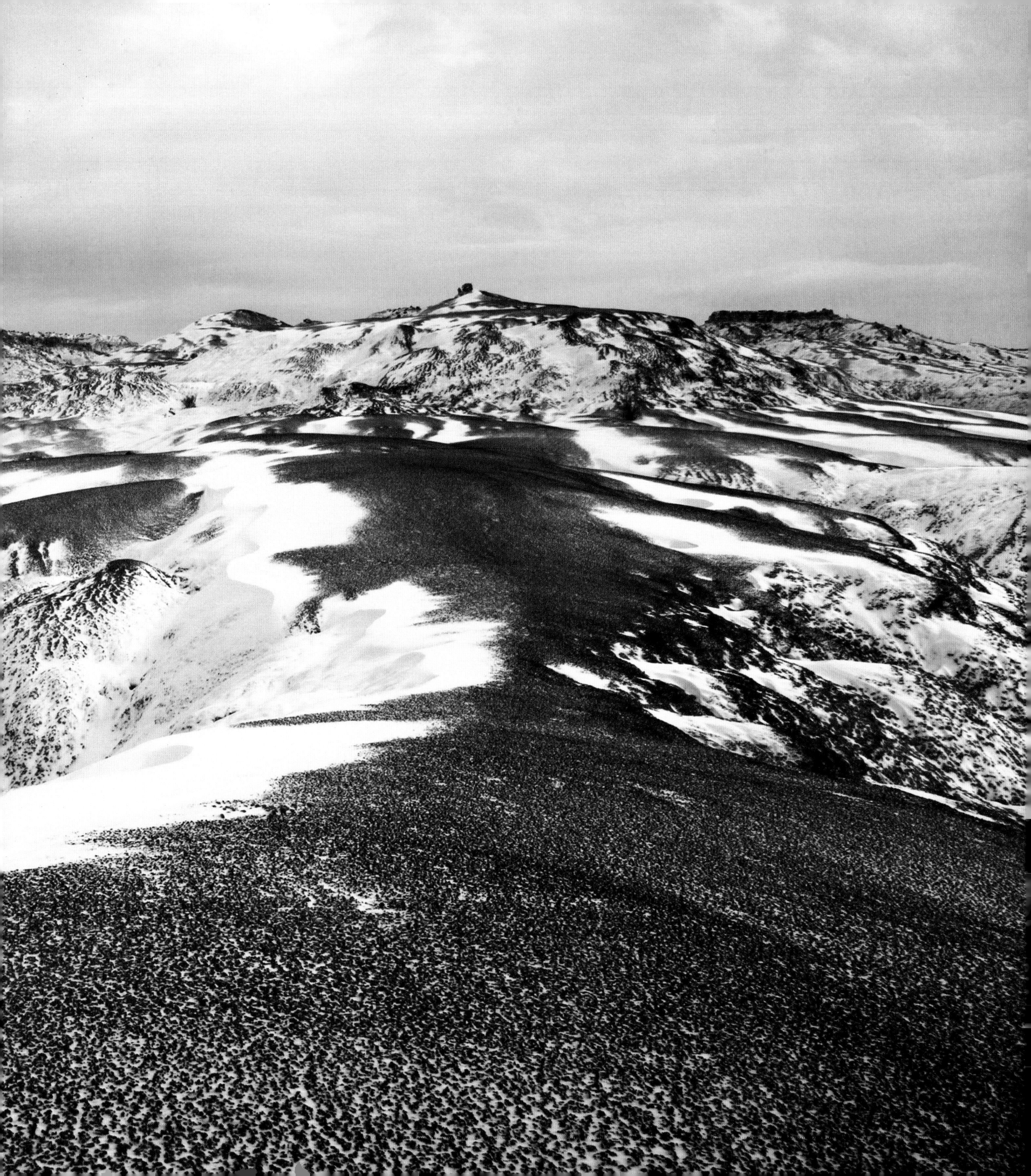

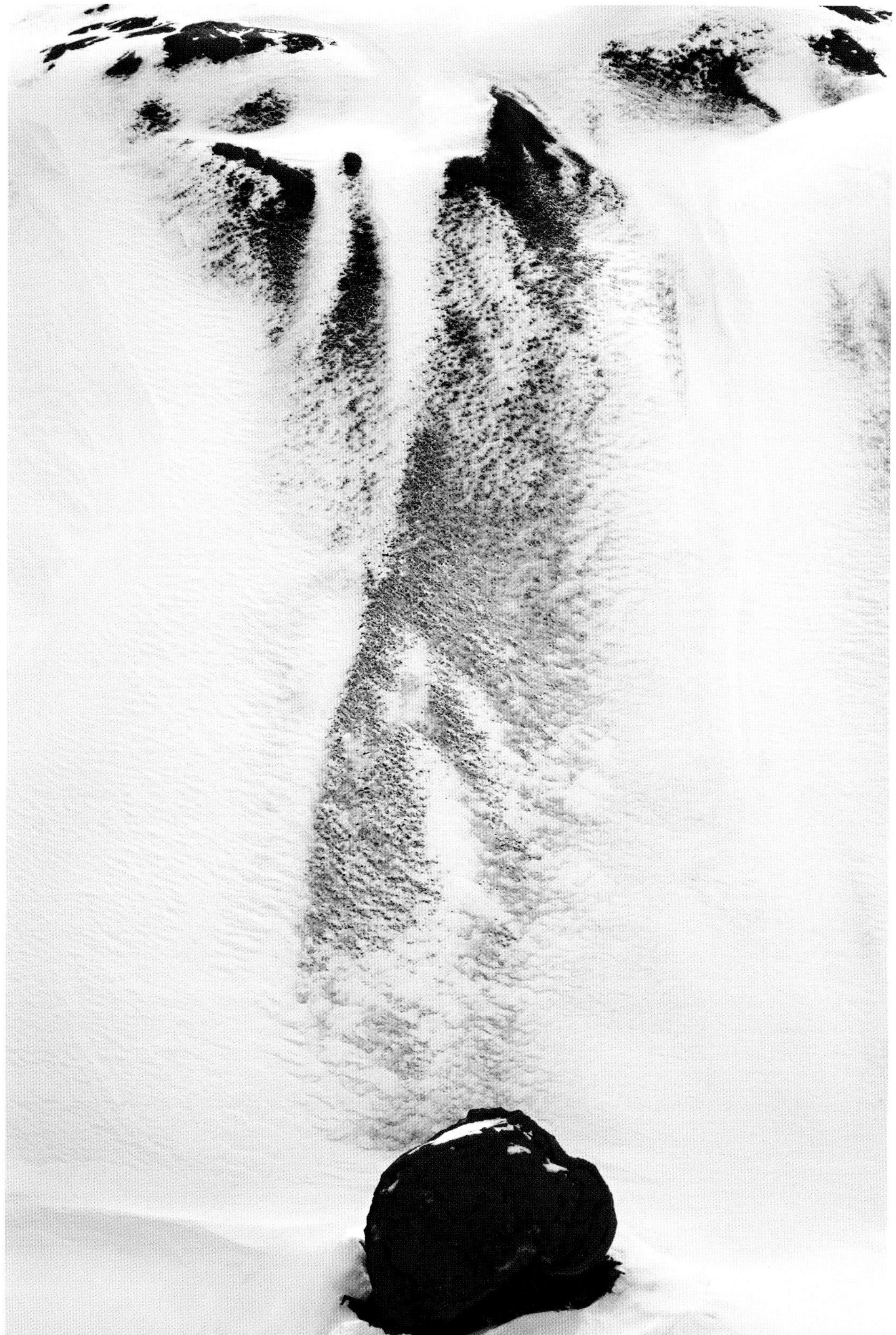

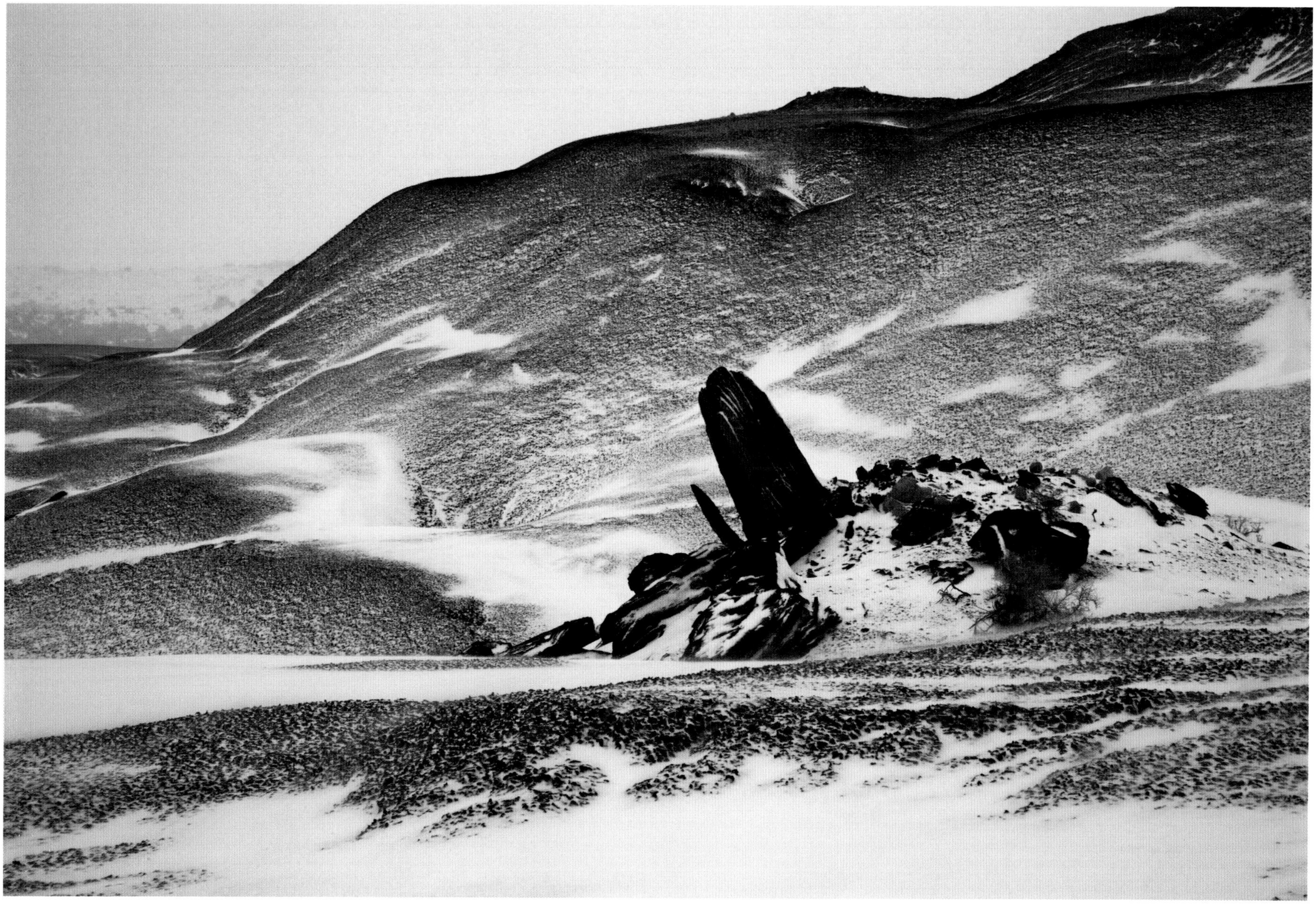

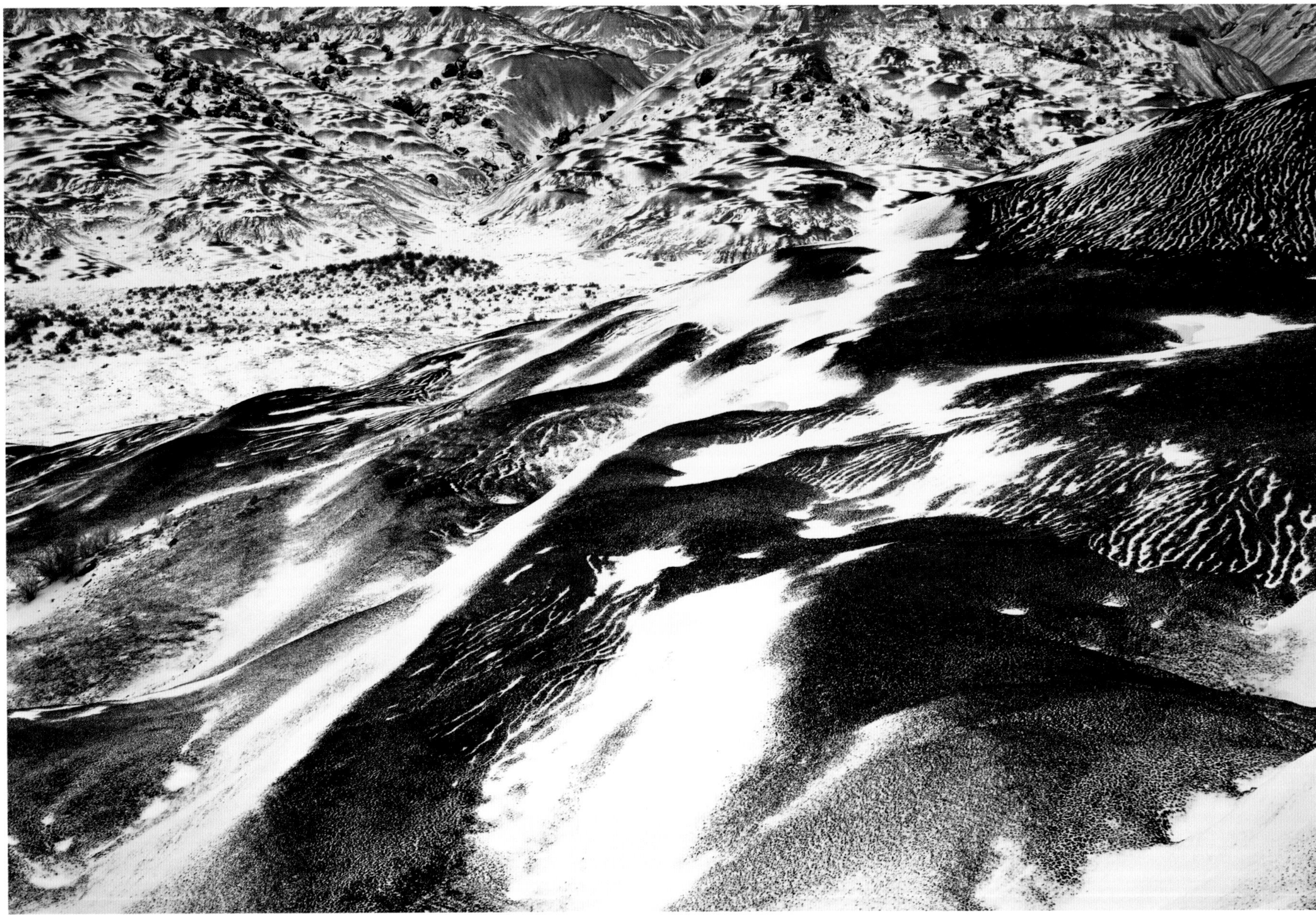

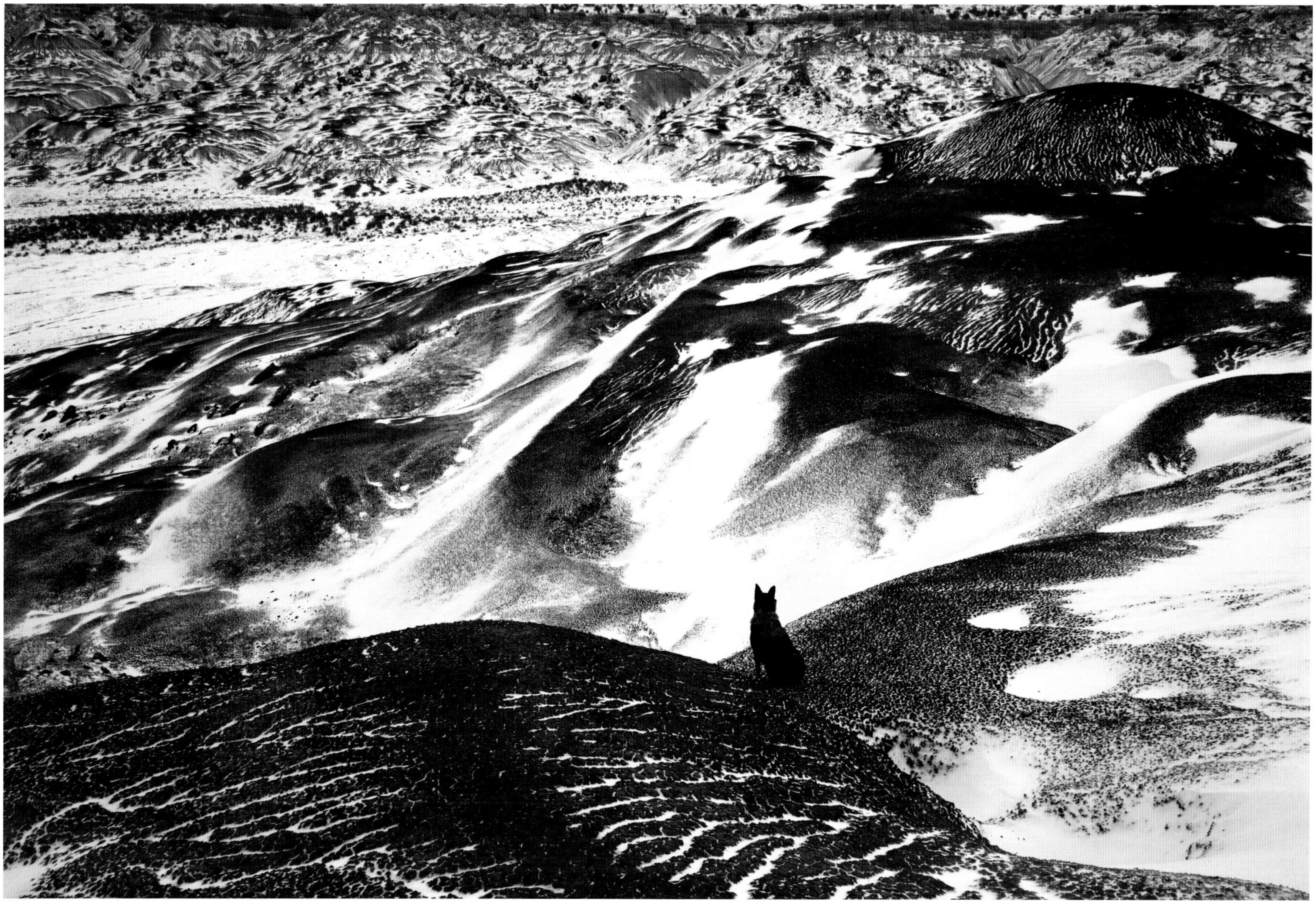

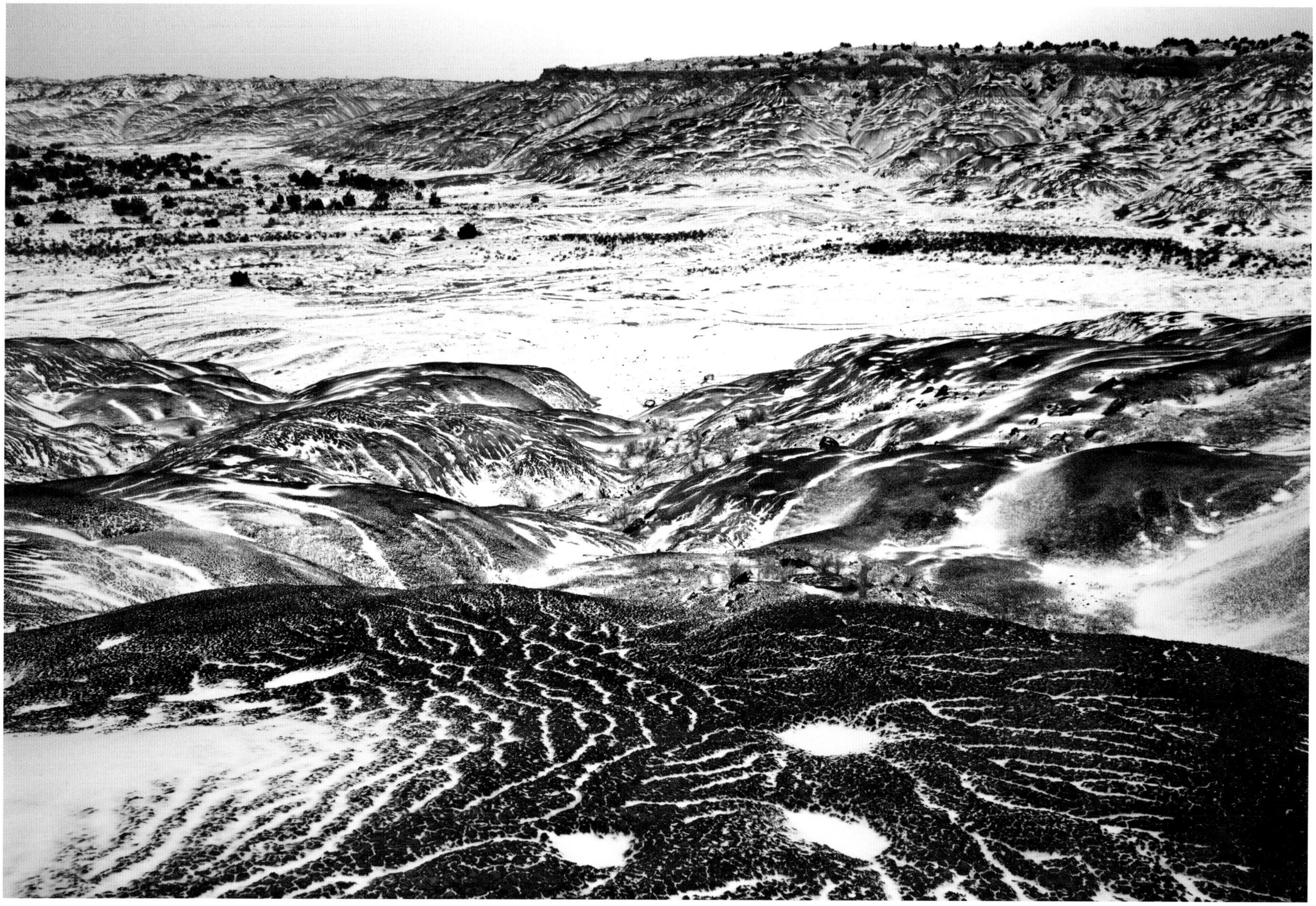

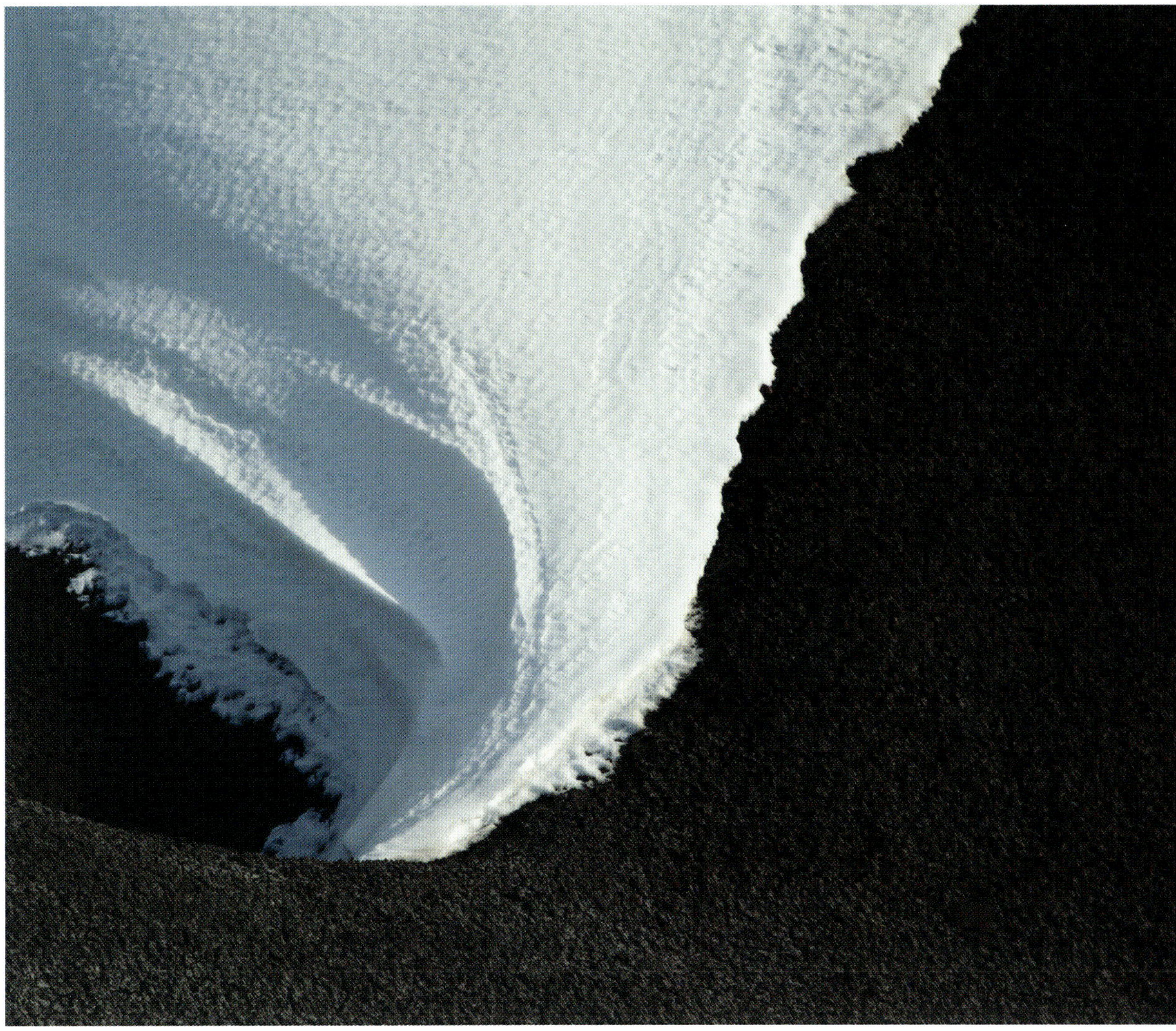

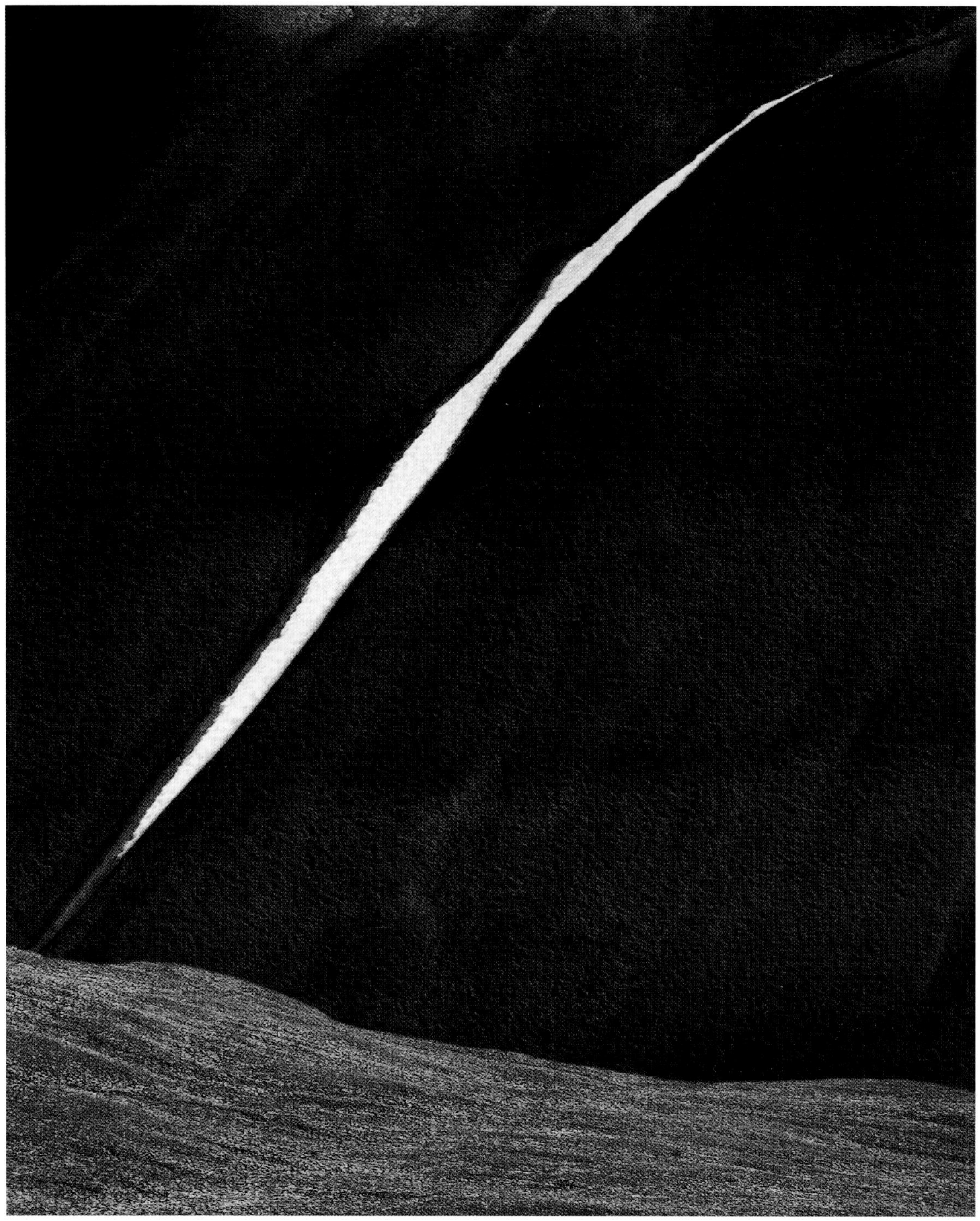

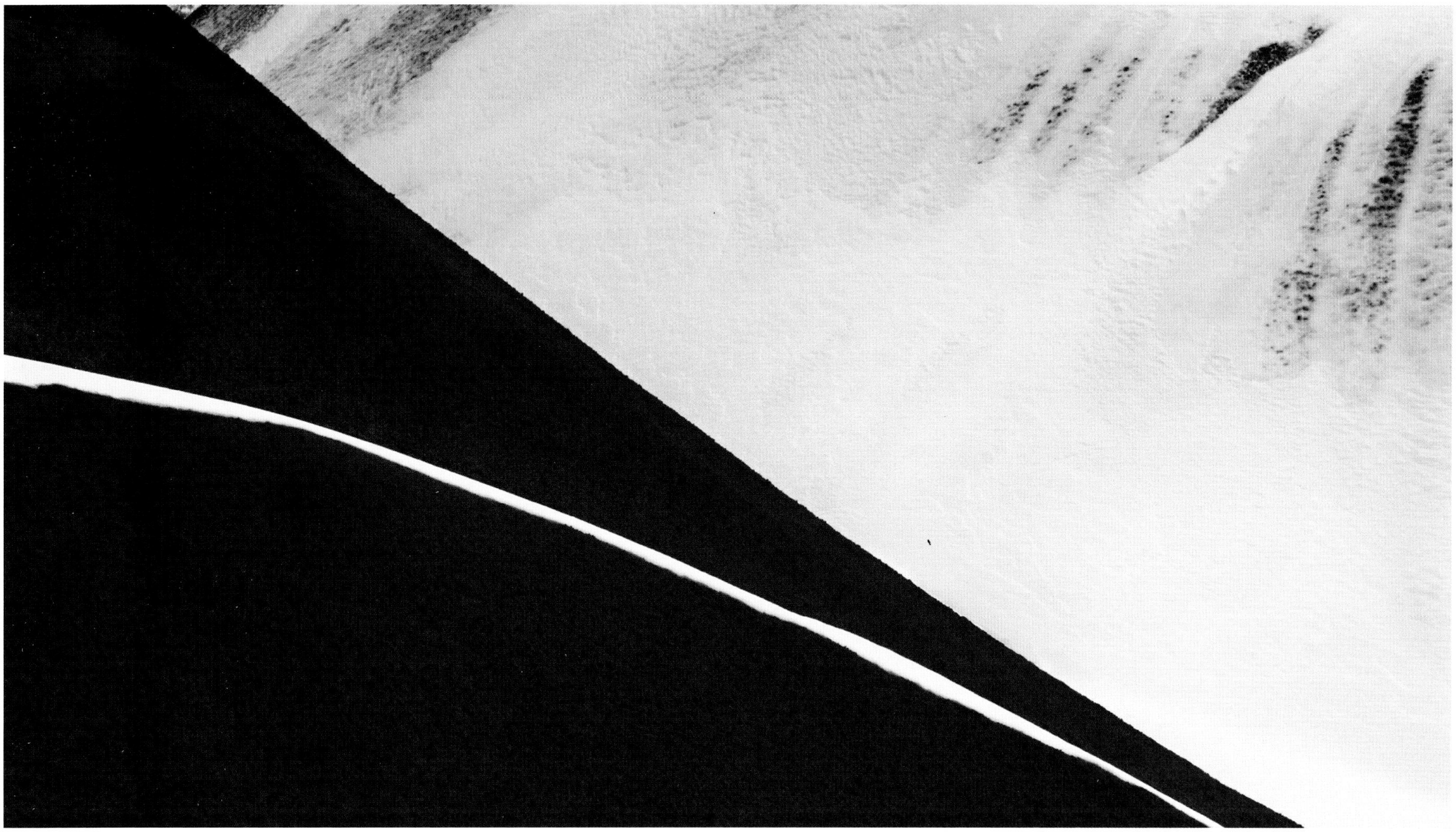

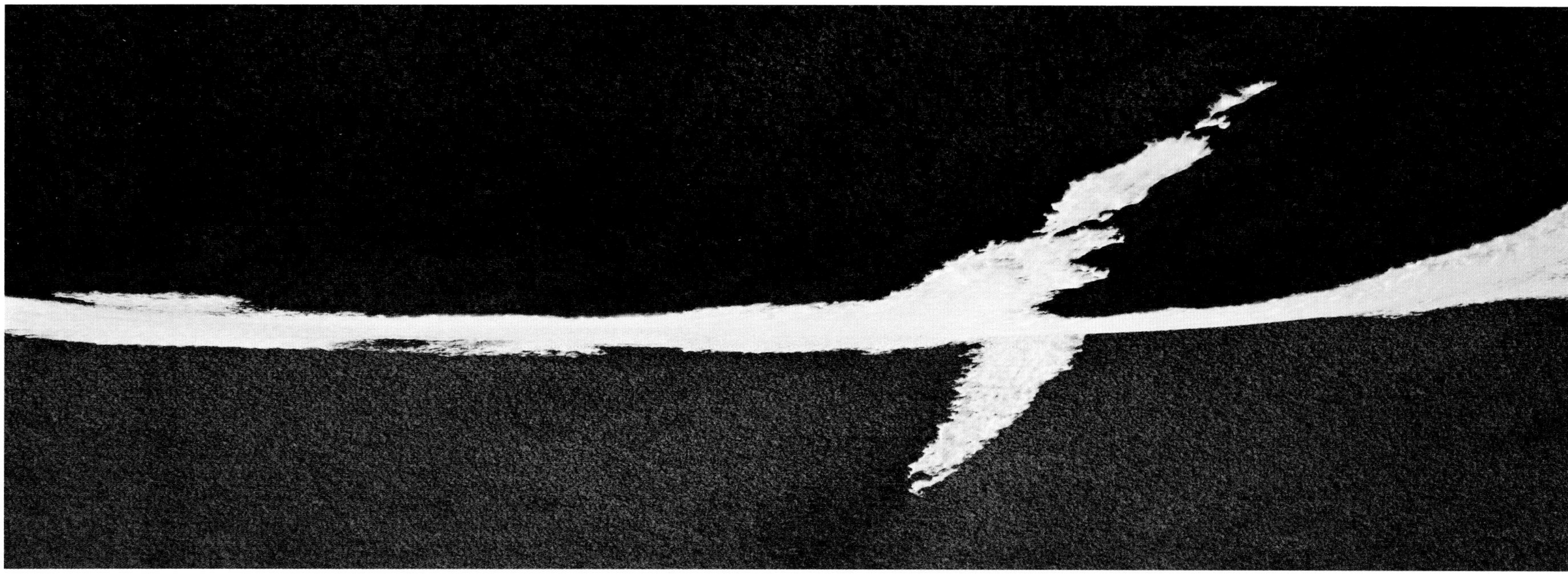

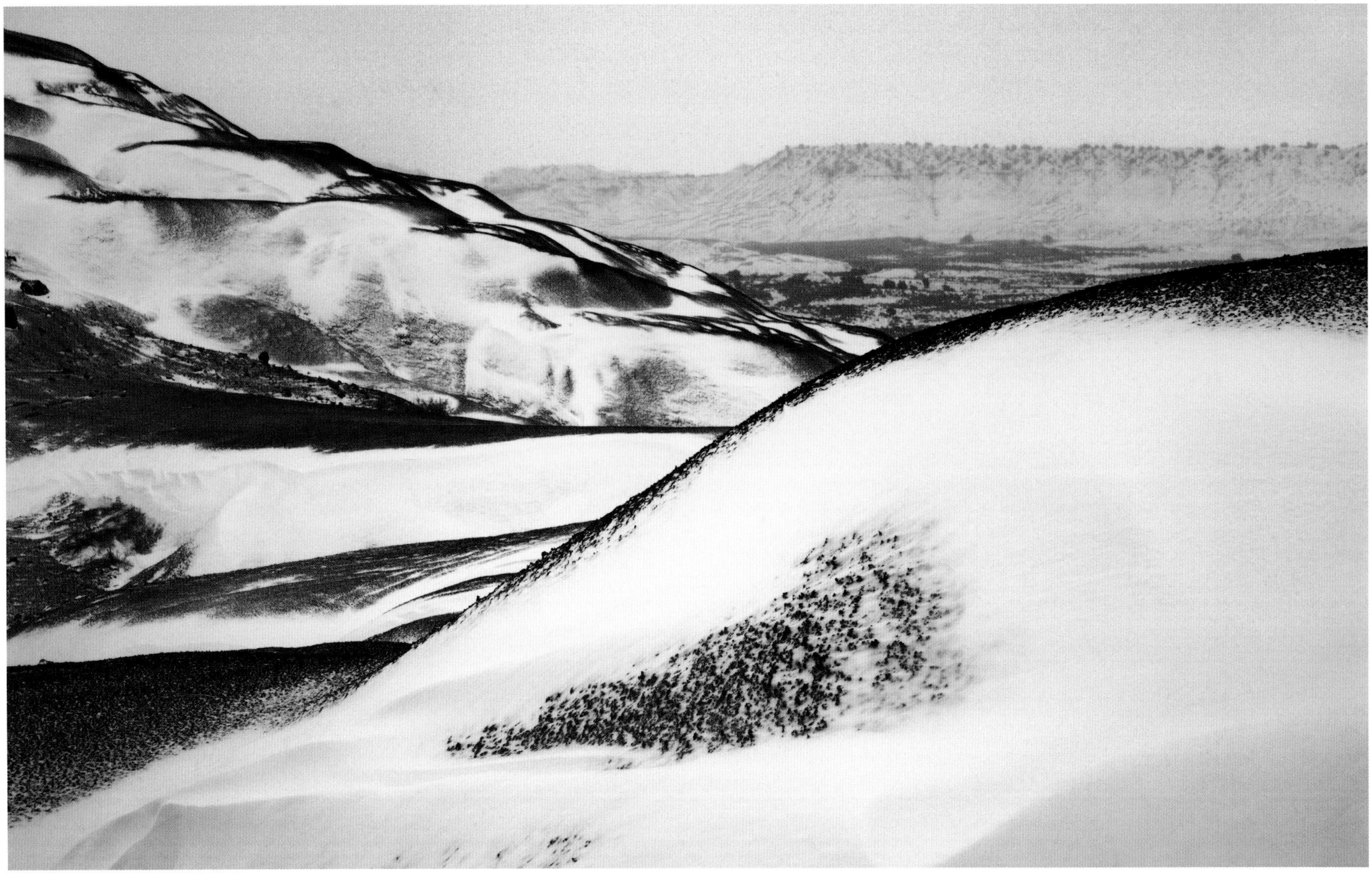

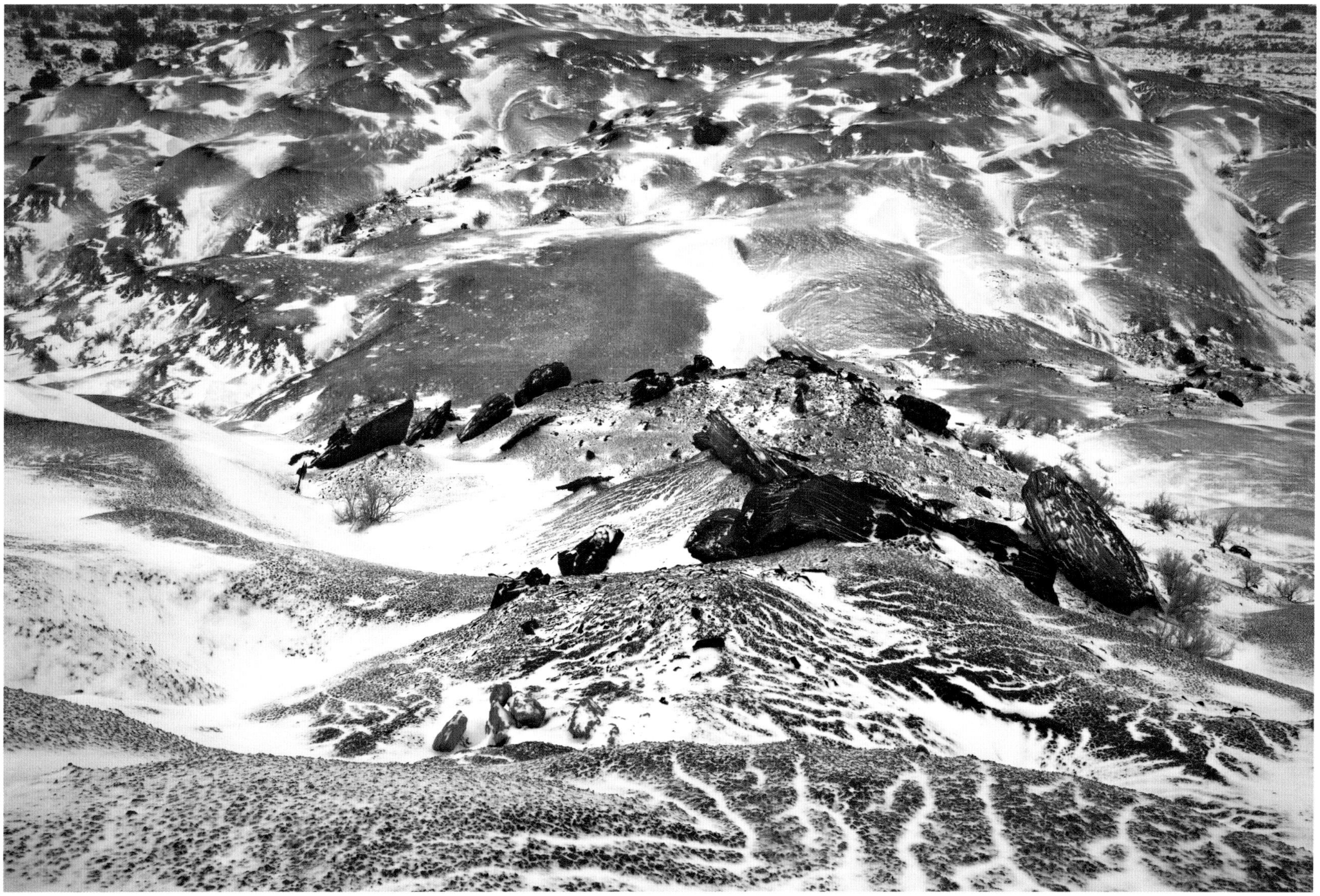

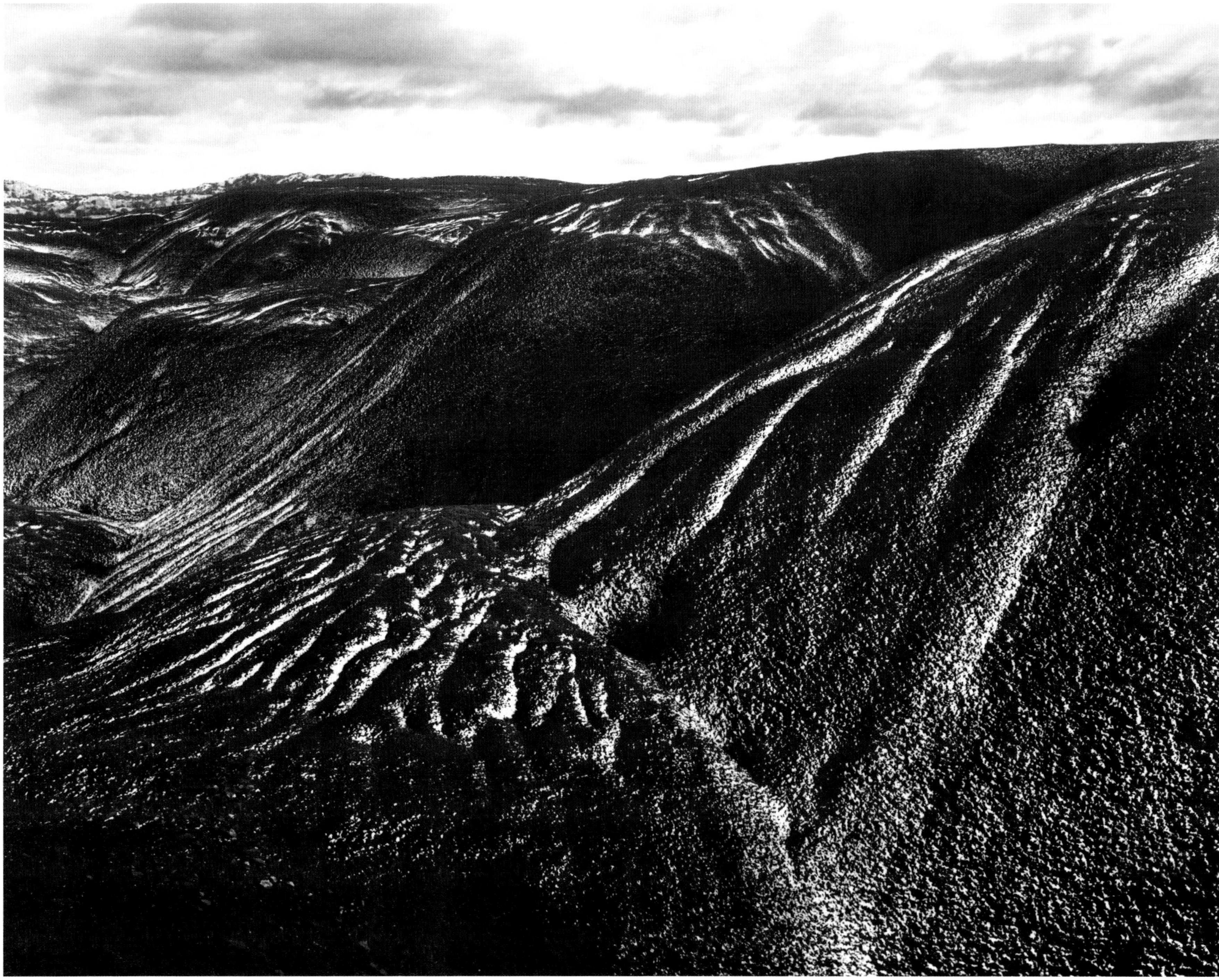

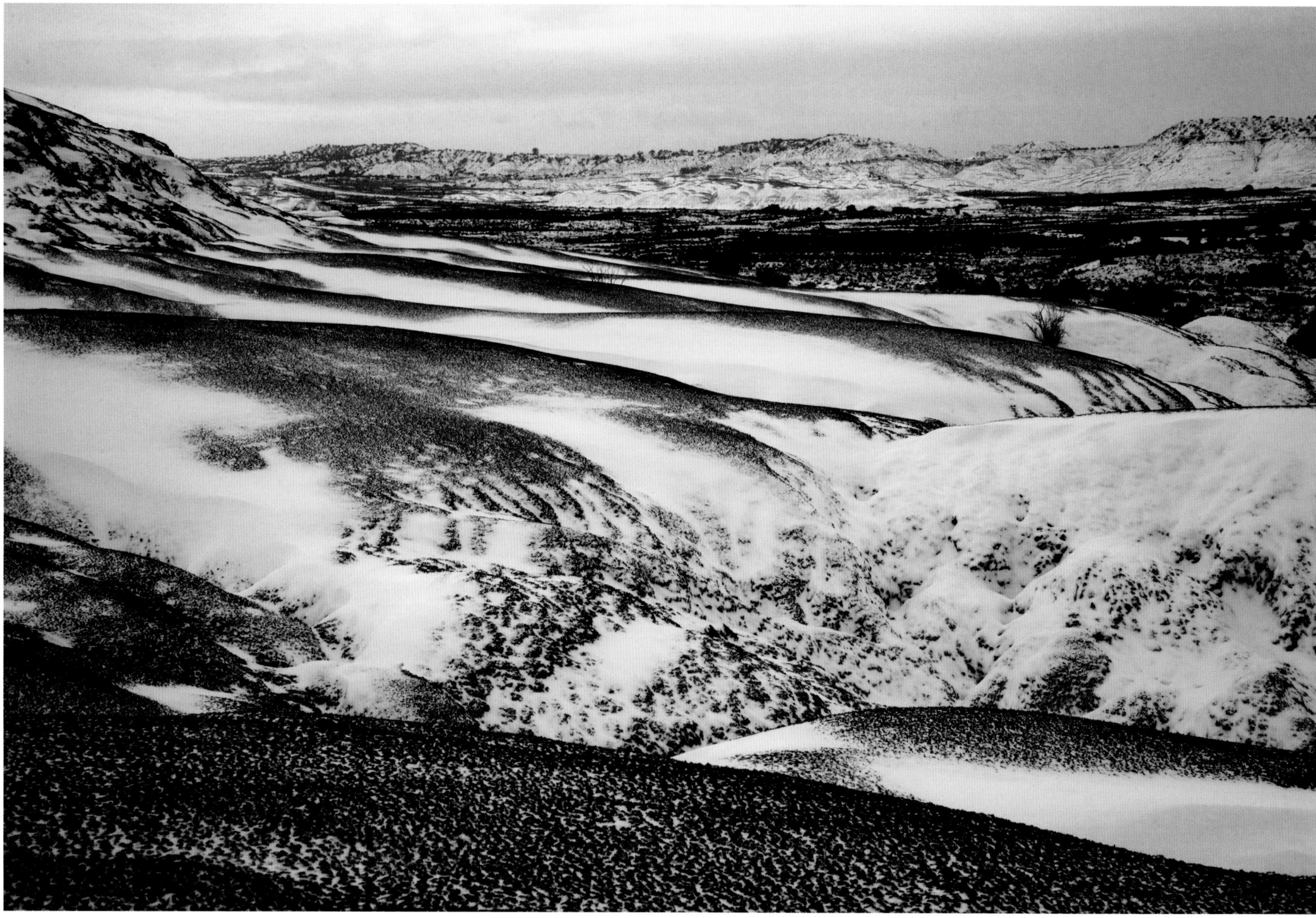

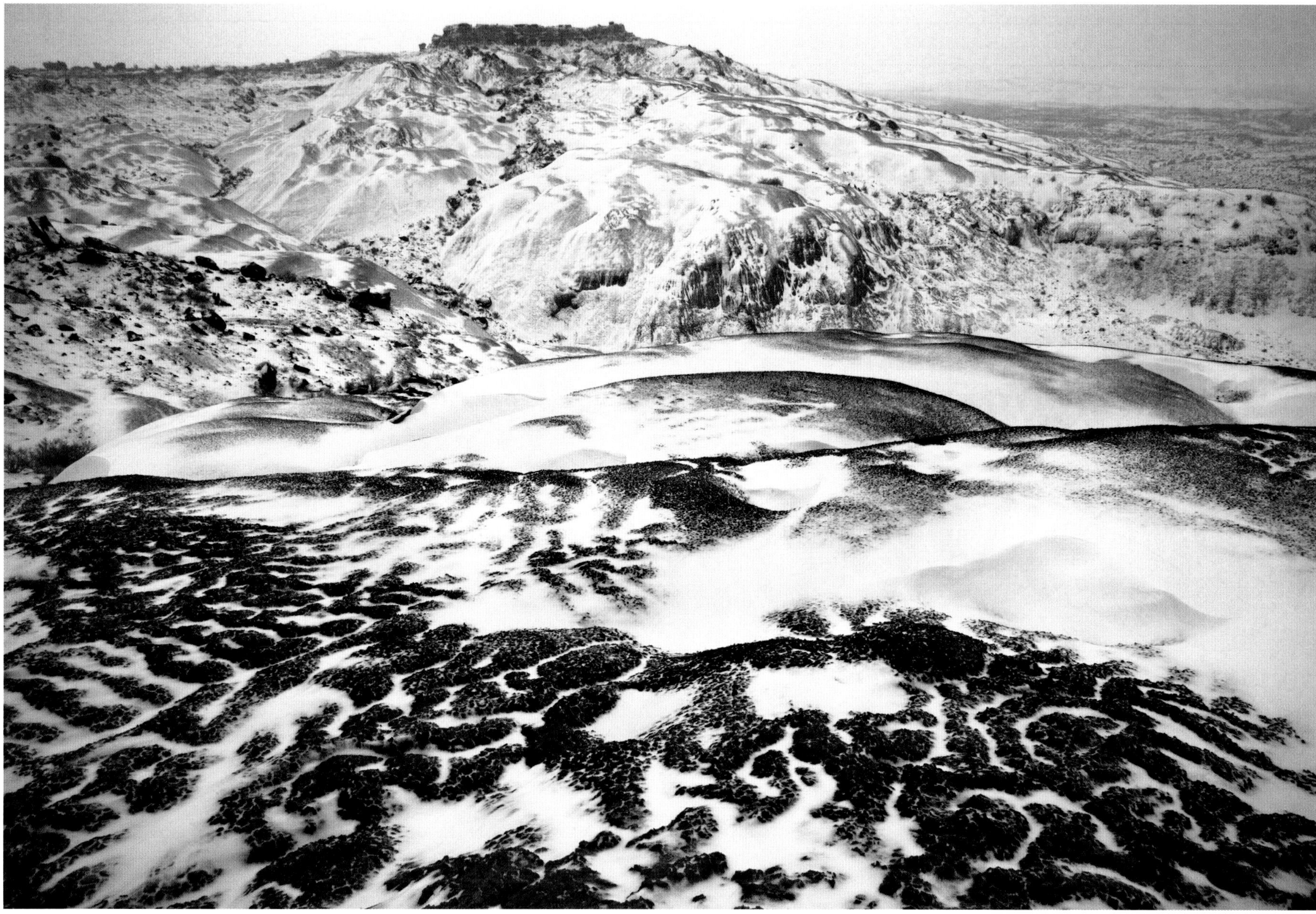

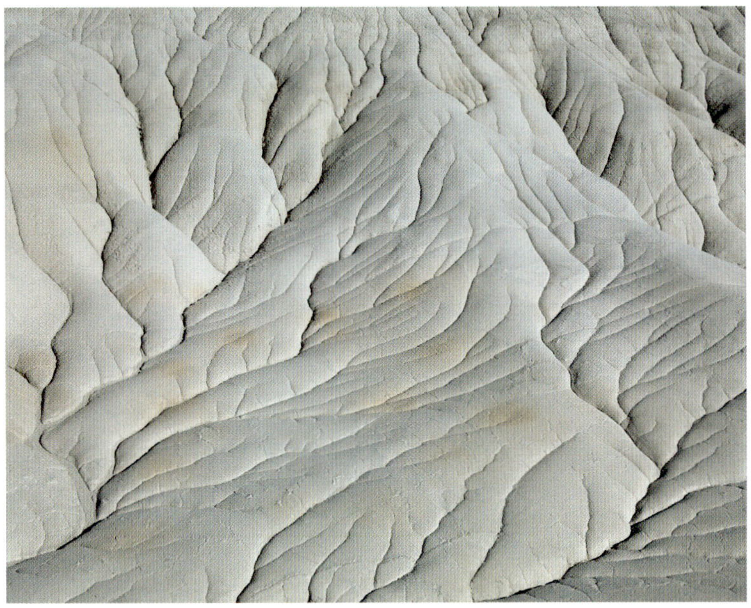
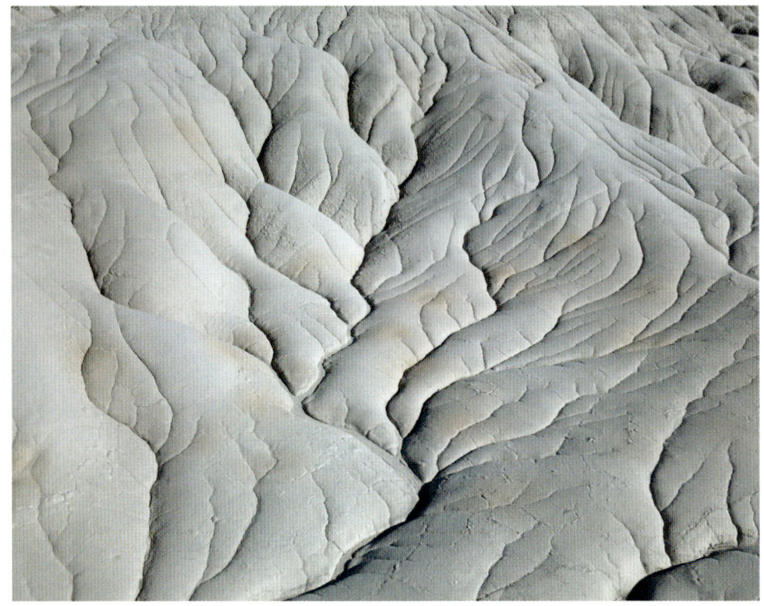
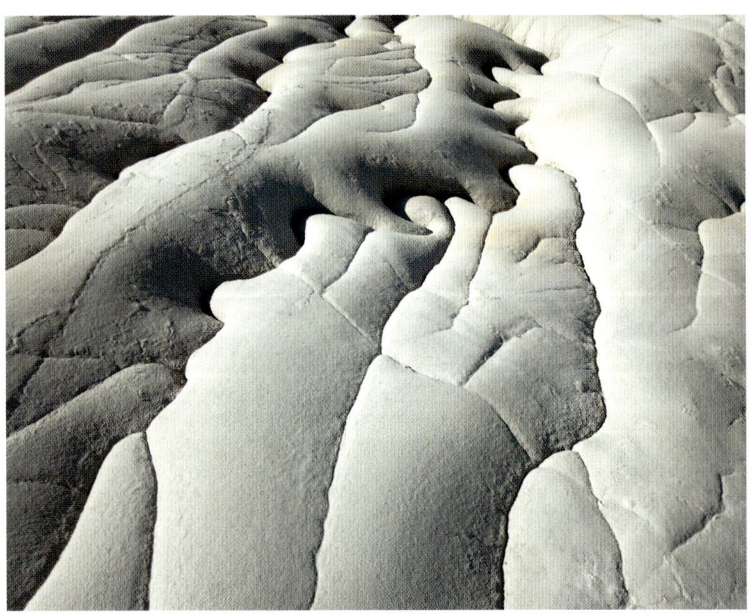
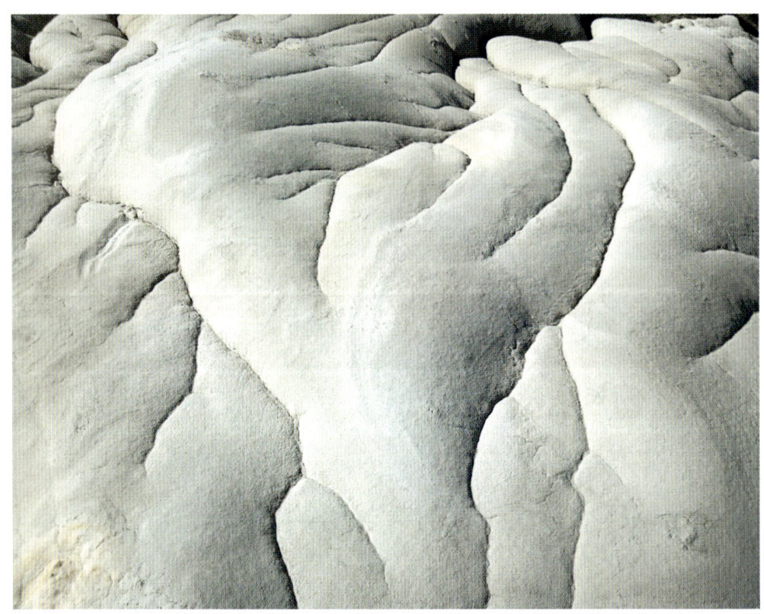

O'KEEFFE'S GHOST

SCIENCE, ART, AND MYSTERY IN THE BLACK PLACE

DOUGLAS PRESTON

IN 1947 A PALEONTOLOGIST from the American Museum of Natural History, Edwin H. Colbert, discovered a remarkable dinosaur graveyard on Ghost Ranch, only two miles from Georgia O'Keeffe's house. It was the largest concentration of complete dinosaur skeletons ever found in the New World, and they were uncovered in the very red hills that O'Keeffe loved to paint. She was fascinated by the discovery and became close friends with Colbert. She often visited the site to watch the scientists at work, and she questioned Colbert closely about what life was like millions of years ago, when Ghost Ranch was a swampy, tropical environment. Dozens of blocks of stone containing the dinosaur bones were packed in wooden crates and shipped back to the museum in New York. One of those blocks ended up forgotten in the museum's basement and sat there gathering dust until 2006, when a curious graduate student chiseled it open to see what was inside. It revealed not a fossilized dinosaur but a rare and fabulous new species of archosaur, a fleet reptile about the size of a dog, dating back 200 million years. Paleontologists at the museum named it *Effigia okeeffeae*, "O'Keeffe's ghost." She is the only artist, to my knowledge, who has had a fossil named after her. I think she would be pleased.

Georgia O'Keeffe had a great affinity for geology. Her landscapes are so accurately observed, so close to nature, that a geologist looking at them would have no trouble naming the geological formations in them. No matter how much O'Keeffe transformed and abstracted the landscape in her work, she never departed from the geological reality of what she observed. She was visually enthralled by land that had been stripped to its bones, eroded to its very soul; she loved the raw hills, the naked badlands, the bare rocks and echoing canyons of the American Southwest.

The most remarkable landscape Georgia O'Keeffe ever painted was the Black Place, a remote, windswept, lifeless range of hills and gullies on the Navajo Indian Reservation. Orville Cox, a cowboy at Ghost Ranch, probably introduced her to the Black Place in 1935 or 1936. She didn't realize that it was already one of the most important geological and paleontological localities in America. She knew only that she had discovered a landscape of enormous significance to her own artistic vision. Over the succeeding four decades, she visited the Black Place many times. These trips resulted in an extraordinary outpouring of brilliant work—drawings, pastels, and oils—that included some of the greatest landscape paintings ever done by an American artist. Her last visit to the Black Place occurred in the mid-1970s, when she was almost ninety years old, half-blind, enfeebled, and requiring assistance. This gives an idea of just how much this place meant to her.

The Black Place has a history dating back 66 million years, to the time when the Chicxulub asteroid slammed into Earth and caused the mass extinction of the dinosaurs. This event opened up a brave new world of evolutionary possibility for the tiny, rodent-like mammals that scurried about the feet of the dinosaurs. The Black Place formed right after this cataclysm, at the very dawn of the Age of Mammals. It is part of what geologists call the Nacimiento Formation, named after a nearby mountain range. It comprises the richest fossil beds of early mammals ever found on Earth.

Sixty million years ago, the Black Place was a huge, stately forest of magnolias, figs, and other flowering trees, growing in a hot and humid environment. It probably looked something like the virgin forests and swamps of Mississippi and Alabama. The forested plains were crisscrossed with enormous rivers, some as big as the Mississippi, which flowed from the north and east, carrying along sediments from the newborn Rocky Mountains. At this time, the Rockies were a humble range of hills only a few thousand feet high, which were slowly being forced up by plate tectonics into the lofty mountains we see today. The rivers wound among floodplains, mudflats, swamps, and shallow lakes in what would become the Black Place. These environments were teeming with fish, fearsome crocodiles, giant turtles, worm lizards, snakes, birds, and the earliest mammals. These mammals had not had time to evolve into larger creatures, and none was bigger than a German shepherd. Among them was a formidable group of animals known as creodonts, the precursors of the true carnivores. The creodonts looked like thick-necked hyenas, with huge, bone-crushing jaws and vicious teeth. A group of cuddly-looking mammals with funny faces and long furry tails, called plesiadapiforms, also lived in these forests. The plesiadapiforms had evolved during the Cretaceous period and were somehow clever enough to have survived the mass extinction. They were cousins or perhaps even the direct ancestors of primates—and as such are part of our own lineage. The plesiadapiforms had the distinction of being the first animals to evolve fingernails in place of claws.

From time to time, while the future Black Place was being formed from layers of sediment, a string of nearby volcanoes would pop off. These eruptions rained ash on the Black Place. The rivers also carried ash from these eruptions, spreading it across the land in layers of black, slippery clay. For 10 million years, ash, mud, clay, and sand formed a layer cake of sediment thousands of feet thick. Around 50 million years ago, a change took place. The area started uplifting. It would eventually rise from only a few hundred feet above sea level to its present altitude of seven thousand feet. This uplift triggered massive erosion. The layers deposited over the previous 10 million years started to wash away. This went on at a slow pace for millions of years. When the last ice age ended and the Southwest dried out, the erosion increased. The Black Place as it appears today was stripped open and exposed only in the last ten thousand years. It is a young landscape composed of 60-million-year-old rocks.

Why does the Black Place look like it does? The black color itself comes not from carbon or coal but from the volcanic ash that once covered the land. The oxidation of iron and manganese in the ash created intense blacks and browns. The green layers come from ash colored by small amounts of copper. The stark white areas are the remains of the ancient riverbeds themselves, which deposited layers of clean quartz sand amid the black. Various minerals in the ash deposits also caused the purple, reddish, and yellowish bands. The highest layer, a bright yellow sandstone intermixed with pebbles, was an ancient river-

Georgia O'Keeffe Rock, *Summer 2012. O'Keeffe was once photographed on this rock (foreground, left), which enabled researchers to determine the location where the artist camped. Her painting* Black Place II *(page 9) came from the formation directly above the rock (see also photograph on page 11).*

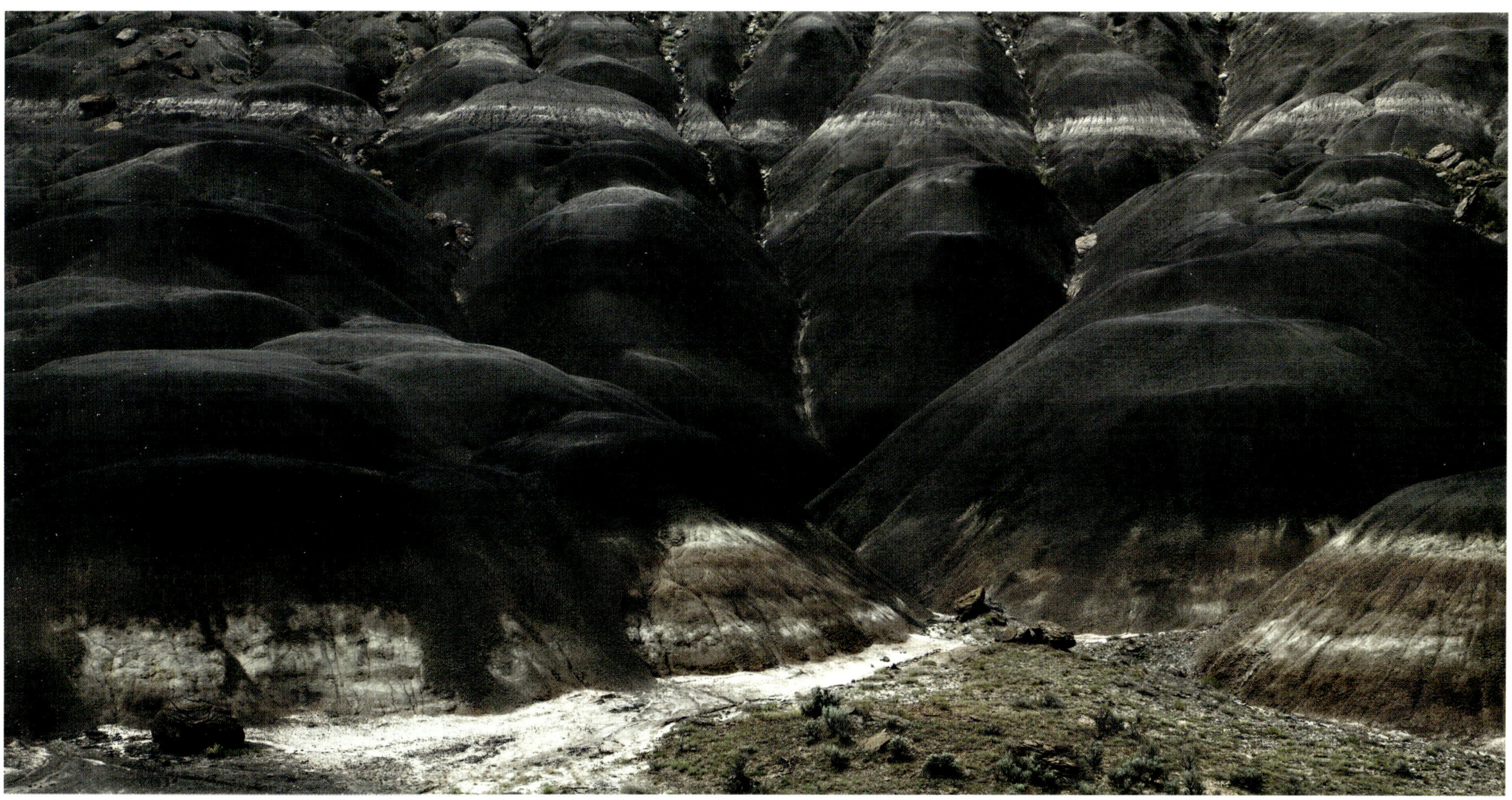

bed, with the color caused once again by the oxidation of trace amounts of iron in the sand.

The surface of the Black Place has a bizarre, cracked, lumpy consistency caused by an unusual mineral called montmorillonite clay. This clay expands when it gets wet and contracts when it dries. Over many years, this process of expansion and contraction creates a texture that geologists call popcorn. When wet, this clay becomes so greasy and slick that it is virtually impossible to walk on it. A single footprint in the wet popcorn may take ten years or more to disappear. It is a fragile environment.

In the photographs you can see peculiar white streaks coming out of the black formations. These are phosphatic and gypsum deposits, some of which originated as fossilized trees. In some areas of the Black Place you can see giant, fossilized tree trunks and root systems, the remains of the vast forests that once covered this land. The floor of the Black Place is littered with yellow and red jasper, along with countless pieces of petrified wood mingled with other tumbled stones. Most of these rocks were washed down from the uplifting of the Rocky Mountains, worn smooth by their long journey rolling along river bottoms in the current. These stones are perhaps 100 million years older than the Black Place itself.

For millennia, Native Americans searched the Black Place for petrified wood, agate, and chert. Here and there, along the flats, you can find a scattering of flakes on the ground—marking a place where an Indian, a thousand or more years ago, paused to flake out an arrowhead or spear point, leaving behind the detritus of his tool-making effort. The ruins of Chaco Canyon lie only twenty-five miles from the Black Place, and the same long drought that drove the Ancient Puebloans from Chaco also turned the Black Place into the lifeless zone you see today.

Some of America's greatest paleontologists collected fossils in the Nacimiento Formation, of which the Black Place is a part. These included William Diller Matthew and George Gaylord Simpson, who worked for the American Museum of Natural History in New York City. Matthew and Simpson scoured the area for fossils in the 1920s and early '30s. While pondering these mysterious badlands, Matthew had the stunning realization that the standard geological history had to be missing an entire age—the very dawn of the Age of Mammals. Matthew named it the Paleocene epoch, thus defining that crucial period when mammals came to rule the planet.

The Black Place is one of the harshest, most unforgiving environments in the country, swept by ferocious winds year-round. It receives only about four inches of rain a year and is almost devoid of life. Temperatures range from over a hundred degrees in summer to twenty below zero in winter. A single day can see a temperature swing of seventy degrees. It was an inhospitable place for O'Keeffe and those before her. The wind often prevented her from painting, threatening to carry away her canvases. It was and still is uninhabited, even by the Navajos on whose land it lies. In the 1930s it was accessible from Ghost Ranch only via a brutal one-hundred-mile drive over dirt roads. The round-trip journey was too long to make in a day, so O'Keeffe would camp out, often with her friend Maria Chabot and sometimes with photographer Eliot Porter. Camping was essential for her painting: it allowed her to be there at dawn and dusk, the best times to paint, when the heat abated, the wind dropped, and the light was richer. She slept in a homemade tent of tarps draped over a frame and would sometimes crawl under her car for shade when the midday sun became unbearable. The paleontologists also found it a difficult landscape, which yielded up its fossil treasures only with effort. When Simpson was a field assistant to Matthew, he wrote a letter complaining about the frustrations of wandering the badlands: "I've been digressing all over the landscape. . . . Now & then we find a fossil—every third day or so, if small fragments count. . . . Poor Dr. Matthew gets madder & madder."

The Black Place has a deep geological, paleontological, and human history. Georgia O'Keeffe sensed the infinitude and mystery in these dark badlands. They inspired her greatest landscape paintings, just as they stimulated the geologists who came before her and the photographers who came after.

This is the landscape that inspired the photographs in this volume, taken by Walter W. Nelson over a period of thirty years. While Nelson originally found the Black Place by following in O'Keeffe's footsteps, these photographs are not a documentation of O'Keeffe's work or an attempt to re-create her vision. Nelson brought his own striking visual expression to these badlands, one that is quite different from O'Keeffe's. His are self-contained works of art that require no reference back to O'Keeffe. These photographs, veering from the surreal to the abstract, capture a different but equally valid spirit of the Black Place. This is what makes the Black Place unique. Artists, scientists, and photographers have all carried away from this landscape their own profound revelations, all different and yet all true. There is no place like it in America.

SOURCES CONSULTED BY DOUGLAS PRESTON

American Museum of Natural History. "Toothless Crocodile Relative, 210 Million Years Old, Walked on Two Feet." Undated press release. http://www.amnh.org/science/papers/crocodile.php.

Colbert, Edwin H. *The Little Dinosaurs of Ghost Ranch*. New York: Columbia University Press, 1995.

Laporte, Leo F. "George Gaylord Simpson (1902–1984)." *GSA Today* (September 2004).

Lucas, Spencer G. Interview with the author, March 2013.

Lynes, Barbara Buhler, Lesley Poling-Kempes, and Frederick W. Turner. *Georgia O'Keeffe and New Mexico: A Sense of Place*. 3rd ed. Princeton, NJ: Princeton University Press, 2004.

Nesbitt, Sterling. "The Anatomy of *Effigia Okeeffeae* (Archosauria, Suchia), Theropod-like Convergence, and the Distribution of Related Taxa." *Bulletin of the American Museum of Natural History* 302 (2007): 1–84.

Poling-Kempes, Lesley. *Ghost Ranch*. Tucson: University of Arizona Press, 2005.

———. Interview with the author, March 2013.

———. *The Valley of Shining Stone: The Story of Abiquiu*. Tucson: University of Arizona Press, 1997.

THIS BOOK IS DEDICATED TO DAVID & LORINE GIBSON
AND MARTHA FAIN

ACKNOWLEDGMENTS

The author would like to acknowledge the following people whose great generosity and support made this book possible:

Ellen Randall, in honor of Annie B. McClintock
and Caren H. Prothro

John Hirschi, Wichita Falls Area Community Foundation

The Kadane Foundation

David Gibson

Martha Fain

Haila Harvey

Annett and Jim Cox

Adriane Arnold

Eugenia Harris

and a special thank you to Gil LaRochelle

Project editor: Mary Wachs

Design and production: David Skolkin

Composition: Set in Sabon with Trajan display.

Manufactured in China

10 9 8 7 6 5 4 3 2 1

Library of Congress Cataloging-in-Publication data
Nelson, Walter W. (Photographer)
[Photographs. Selections]
The Black Place—two seasons / photographs by Walter W. Nelson ; introduction by Katherine Ware ; essay by Douglas Preston.
pages cm
Includes bibliographical references.
ISBN 978-0-89013-587-7
1. Bisti/De-Na-Zin Wilderness (N.M.)—Pictorial works. 2. Mountains—New Mexico—Pictorial works. 3. Landscape photography. 4. Repeat photography. 5. O'Keeffe, Georgia, 1887-1986--Homes and haunts—New Mexico—Pictorial works. I. Title.
F802.A16N45 2014
978.9'82—DC23
2013035704

Museum of New Mexico Press
PO Box 2087
Santa Fe, New Mexico 87504
mnmpress.org

PAGE 6

#1, *Spring, Summer, Fall,* Series I, 2012, 40½ x 33½ x 2½ in., black and white earth in medium, red jasper, oil on wood

#2, *Winter,* Series I, 2012, 40½ x 33½ x 2½ in., black and white earth in medium, red jasper, oil on wood

#1, *Spring, Summer, Fall,* Series II, 2012, 40½ x 33½ x 2½ in., black and white earth in medium, red jasper, oil on wood

#2, *Winter,* Series II, 2012, 40½ x 33½ x 2½ in., black and white earth in medium, red jasper, oil on wood

PAGE 9

Georgia O'Keeffe, American (Sun Prairie, Wisconsin 1887–1986 Santa Fe, New Mexico). *Black Place II, 1944.* Oil on canvas, 23⅞ x 30 inches (60.6 x 76.2 cm.).The Metropolitan Museum of Art, Alfred Stieglitz Collection, 1959 (59.204.1). © The Metropolitan Museum of Art. Photo: Malcom Varon. Photo credit: Image copyright © The Metropolitan Museum of Art. Image source: Art Resource, NY.